In the Shadow of the Holocaust

Events and Ideologies
Confronting an Immigrant
to the United States

Ludwig L. Geismar, Ph.D.

VANTAGE PRESS
New York

Cover design by Susan Thomas

FIRST EDITION

All rights reserved, including the right of
reproduction in whole or in part in any form.

Copyright © 2005 by Ludwig L. Geismar, Ph.D.

Published by Vantage Press, Inc.
419 Park Ave. South, New York, NY 10016

Manufactured in the United States of America
ISBN: 0-533-15021-3

Library of Congress Catalog Card No.: 2004096267

0 9 8 7 6 5 4 3 2 1

In memory of my parents and brother Siegbert

Contents

Preface   vii

1. My Enemy's Enemy Is My Friend   1
2. Confusing Signals in a Free Society   32
3. Zionism, Reactive and Proactive   53
4. The Rhythm of Army Life: "Hurry Up and Wait"   67
5. Reflections on What Used to Be Home   84
6. Anzio—A Mediterranean Beachhead   95
7. War from a Different Perspective   106
8. The Screening of Post-War America—
   A View from the Campus   125
9. Life in the Young Jewish State   148

Afterword   187
Bibliography   193

Preface

The narrative of this book represents a memoir of the first decades of my life. In writing it, I responded to requests by my children and grandchildren to share with them experiences that have aroused their curiosity. Their interest, in addition to being part of the family, comes from exposure to information about Nazi anti-Semitism, the Holocaust, World War II, and the birth of Israel. For better or worse, most of my early life intertwined with all of these. So I chose to put together a written account that covers adolescence as a Jew in Germany, loss of both parents and brother, and nearly all my uncles, aunts, and cousins in the Holocaust; immigration to the United States; overseas service in the U.S. Army; university education in America and Israel, and return to the U.S. for an academic career.

How then, it may be asked, does writing of a memoir intersect with a focus on ideology as indicated in the book's title? As far back as age fourteen, after the rise of the German National Socialists to power, one of the most significant events in my life was membership in the Zionist youth movement. I still vividly recall the importance of my movement's ideology, countering the one imposed by the state. In subsequent years—immigration to the United States without my parents, adjustment to a totally new environment, service in the army, college studies in two countries, living with my own family in the newly established State of Israel—all of these constituted new ideological encounters. Each called for a sorting out of ideas as a means of understanding life around me. It is this sifting process which, speaking for myself, appeared to be so essential for coming to terms with people and events. Does it seem far-fetched to think that others might find it similarly meaningful to examine one's experiences in the context of ideological encounters? The reader will have to judge.

In this country, the term ideology carries a negative connotation, because people link it to the word ideologue denoting a person who rigidly and uncritically advocates certain beliefs. There is arguably another explanation, namely the nature of the U.S. two-party system, which puts less emphasis than many European political systems on articulated theories of governance. American politics puts greater stress on personality and appearance, particularly on television. With more parties in the running in many foreign countries, ideologies serve invariably as labels for differentiating political parties. There might even be a factual basis for the old stereotype that holds that the difference between U.S. Democrats and Republicans is that between Tweedledee and Tweedledum.

From a social science perspective ideologies are viewed both in a negative and positive light. Daniel Bell (1962) put the subject on a high-profile map in the 1960s with his book *The End of Ideology* which called for terminating the passionate rhetoric and expressed the hope that its place would be taken by pragmatic discourse which leaves room for social change and progress. By contrast, Chaim Waxman, in a volume he edited under the title *The End of the Ideology Debate* (1962), expressed the view that we are in need of "a broad plastic ideology which will enable us to transcend our current stagnation."

My personal frame of reference leans toward advocating ideological explorations as a means for sorting out the relationship between ideas and human behavior. I have examined that issue by way of dissertations at the master's as well as doctoral level. The former was devoted to a study of identity feelings among Jewish teenagers relative to their social adjustment (Geismar, 1954); the latter to investigating the relationship between the Zionist ideology among immigrants to Israel (Geismar, 1959). In both (empirical) studies the question concerned the connection between people's beliefs and their adaptation to the social environment.

In the argument between the pro-and-contra ideology groups, I adhere to neither. Following Parsons, I define the concept as a belief system that attempts to understand, explain, and change the world and to which people have a commitment. I am not making a statement about the quality of ideologies. After all, beliefs as diverse as affirmative action, evolution, fascism, free market theory, isolationism, and Zionism can be subsumed under this heading. Their assessment is beyond the scope of this memoir. Instead I am focusing on selected belief systems that had an impact on me in growing up and making my way in diverse cultural settings. In this personal narrative, I wish to share this experience with the reader because I believe that the ideological perspective is a tool for understanding the human experience.

The impetus for this present memoir came partly from an accidental encounter between my daughter Aviva, a modern dancer in New York, and a small group of New York residents with family connections in the German town of Breisach am Rhein. This is the town where my parents and grandparents were born. During the past five years this group had been engaged with a number of Breisach volunteers, led by Dr. Walesch-Schneller, in the Association for the Restoration of Jewish Life. Aviva, bearing her Geismar maiden name, which is very common in the Breisach area, served as a conduit to me, and this resulted in a request from the above association to participate in their activities. They had specifically in mind a visit to commemorate the deportation of Jews, which included my parents, aunts, uncles, and cousins on October 22, 1940 from the provinces bordering the Rhine. The deportation led to camps in Vichy, France and ultimately to Auschwitz and death by gassing.

My contact with the Breisach group was fortuitous. Previous efforts to explore family roots were confined to examining family trees and search for names in rosters produced by the Nazi regime. The Breisach program enabled me to be part of an endeavor that commemorated the lives of loved ones and of millions of innocent victims of the Nazi cataclysm. Breisach also represented an effort on a community level to make Germany and other Axis nations confront their bloody past and struggle to avoid recurrence. This is the larger context within which the story of my life is enveloped in a quest for a brighter future for all.

In the Shadow of
the Holocaust

1

My Enemy's Enemy Is My Friend

I was born in 1921 into a Jewish lower middle-class family in Mannheim, Germany. My parents, both natives of a small German town, Breisach, on the banks of the Rhein river, had married shortly before World War I. They identified themselves as Jews, being members of a "liberal" synagogue, whose practices stood somewhere between those of the American conservative and reform movements. Politically my parents' orientation could best be described as middle of the road, leaning toward conservatism whose guiding themes were continuity and patriotism.

We lived in a working-class neighborhood where my parents had a small shoe store. During my father's army service in World War I, my mother ran the store and took care of my older brother Siegbert, who was born in 1914. My parents' closest social contacts were with relatives, the families of my father's two brothers and my mother's second cousin, all of whom resided in the same city in easy walking distance from our home. One of the uncles, my father's older sibling, Salomon, also owned a store, selling notions, and it was located on the same block as my father's business. The younger brother, Theodor, was a custom tailor. My mother's cousin, Julius, was a manufacturer of work gloves and mittens. His enterprise was notably larger and more successful than that of the three brothers.

The four families had a total of only six children. My uncle Theodor and his wife were childless. My father's brother Salomon had one child who was several years older than my brother. My own family had three children, Siegbert, seven years my senior, myself, and my sister, Hedy, who was three years younger than I. My mother's cousins had boy and girl twins, about my own age (small families were the norm in western Europe during the period between the two world wars).

In the absence of natural family-rooted play groups, we children, when bored, took to visiting relatives whose women were nurturing types and made us feel welcome. The relationship among the families of the brothers was marked by periodic squabbles and bickering, followed by avoidance until someone took the initiative to make up. Socializing took the form of spontaneous visits by the adults, but rarely, dinner invitations or joint holiday celebrations.

My parents made the independence of their children, particularly the boys, an important component of education. This included finding solutions when we got into trouble with others whether at school or outside of school. Since both parents were busy supporting the family we had to look after ourselves during our free time and, not unexpectedly, things would occasionally go wrong. At one time while playing "cowboys" with a grade school friend at my home, I broke a glass lampshade while throwing a lasso. At another time while hanging on to the tailgate of a truck (getting a free ride), the truck accelerated to the point where I chose to jump off. Unfortunately, my trousers got caught on a hook, and in the process of freeing myself I tore them into two. In both instances, my parents showed disapproval but assumed correctly that I had learned my lesson. There was no punishment.

There were other cases of practiced independence where, in retrospect, the option for independence was misplaced. I recall an occasion, when I was seven or eight years old, I was plagued by a bad earache. Intuitively, my mother diagnosed it accurately as a problem with my teeth, and she made an appointment for me with the dentist. She sent me alone because she had to mind the store while my father was on the road as a traveling salesman. This, my first trip ever to a dentist, was marked by the most intense pain I had experienced when his drill touched a raw nerve without anesthetic. When I was nine or ten years old, my parents overestimated my readiness to be a bill collector to liquidate bad debts of store customers. When I received such an assignment, the clients usually ignored my request since the presence of a child posed no threat to their delinquency.

Public school was for me a mixed experience. My parents expected high achievement. My brother, who was exceptionally bright and skipped a grade in elementary school, implicitly set the standards for me. When I entered middle school, my principal teacher, the rough equivalent of the American homeroom teacher, happened to be the same person who taught some of my brother's classes seven years earlier. When he discovered the family connections, his first words to me were, "Your brother was a clever dog, I hope you will do as well as he did."

The beginning of my school career, however, was anything but promising. German elementary schools during the post-war era provided no easing-in process, comparable to the American kindergarten. The program did not leave much room for individual differences in the development of learning skills. For me, Gothic handwriting posed a problem. Every morning, our first-grade teacher lined us up according to the quality of penmanship. The bottom quarter were punished (he must have assumed that ability was distributed on a normal curve), by way of a *Tatze*, a blow on the underside of the fingers with a bamboo stick. My daily reaction to this form of torture was sickness and throwing up before leaving for school. I spent the entire Christmas vacation practicing my handwriting with emotional support from my mother while she was working at the store. Following the vacation, my writing had improved to the point where I not only escaped punishment, but also found myself among the top five or six in first-grade penmanship.

Postscript: Several weeks later I was promoted to the second grade. Our new teacher put much less emphasis on writing and was permissive in other ways as well. My handwriting deteriorated in no time and has not recovered since.

Measuring up to family or academic standards was, however, only a minor problem compared to facing the growing manifestations of anti-Semitism that engulfed more and more segments of German society, including public schools. Prior to the Nazi takeover, offensive remarks by non-Jewish fellow students or exclusion from their informal social groups were experienced by us as minor annoyances that our elders viewed as something we had to live with. A sea change occurred with Hitler's ascendancy to power in January 1933.

At our level, a German middle school, change played itself out by a new regulation barring Jewish students from being officers in student organizations. In view of the fact that I was the class vice-president at that time, our principal teacher had to conduct new elections to have a non-Jewish student take my place. Another regulation that soon followed excluded Jewish students from being given awards for scholastic achievement. This affected my cousin, Hans—now Harry, (the son of Julius), and myself since we were were at the top of the class. As memorable as the exclusion was the principal teacher's statement to the class, when announcing the recipients that "the new regulations unfortunately precluded awards being bestowed on our Jewish students" was gratifying and chilling at the same time. Given the way the Nazi regime dealt with dissent, this was clearly a courageous statement. The two acts of discrimination cited here were part of a policy that led within two years to the complete elimination of all Jewish students from the public school system.

During the period preceding the Nazi takeover my parents were trying to understand what was happening to the country they loved and where their ancestors had lived for centuries. Hitler's plans laid out in *Mein Kampf* were known well enough, but his political career, marked by many early failures, including time spent in jail, seemed to indicate that he was a crackpot who would be held in check by the authorities of the Weimar Republic. In the elections for the *Reichstag* preceding the fraudulent November 1933 plebiscite, the National Socialist Party had fallen short of a majority. In a run-off election for the German presidency, Hitler received only 37 percent of the vote compared to the incumbent von Hindenburg's 53 percent. Among my parents and other German Jews of their generation there was a widespread feeling that the democratic Weimar

Republic was strong enough to survive.

Hitler's assumption of the chancellorship in January 1933 accompanied by emergency decrees suspending constitutional guarantees of free speech, right of assembly, a free press, and rights of privacy, accompanied by the establishment of the first concentration camps, left German Jews in a state of shock. There was little doubt that the Third Reich, a regime of terror, was going to be around for some time to come.

My father pinned his hopes of survival on his contributions to the "fatherland" as a frontline fighter in World War I (the only concession granted to him by his country was an earlier release from imprisonment in the Dachau concentration camp in 1938). Until *Kristallnacht* (the night of the broken glass) on November 9, 1938, there was some hope in my own family that the Nazi tempest would eventually blow over. My mother believed the Nazi regime would not last more than a decade (her prediction, of course was nearly correct, especially when held up against the Nazi plan for a 10,000-year Reich), and she certainly could not conceive of the mass genocide, which at this point was still in the planning stage.

Following my Bar Mitzvah in 1934, I joined an organization that called itself The Jewish Youth Community. Its leader was the charismatic and scholarly Rabbi Max Gruenewald, who was a role model for us not only as an intellectual leader but also as a good soccer player. The Youth Community was loosely organized and held weekly meetings for the most part. I wished at this stage of my life to be part of a group with a more intensive program especially since neither home nor school provided me with the sociability and mental stimulation I needed.

A major change in my life occurred as a result of being

recruited into a youth Zionist movement, called the *Werkleute* (freely translated into Craftsmen). It was a chapter of a German-Jewish youth movement (with a national membership of about 1,000) that came into being when the *Kameraden*, also a German-Jewish youth organization, split into several segments, one of which became the *Werkleute*. The differentiating characteristic of the *Werkleute* was a Zionist orientation meaning preparation for life in a Palestinian (Israeli after statehood in 1948) Kibbutz and resettlement there as soon as feasible.

Some explanation is in order regarding the term youth movement as a historical phenomenon during the first third of the twentieth century. Youth groups, according to the Israeli sociologist Eisenstadt, are structures that link childhood and adulthood to provide for a smoother transition from one life-cycle stage to another. He argued, furthermore, that the greater the complexity in society and the more pronounced the gaps among generations, the greater the likelihood that youth groups will emerge (Eisenstadt, 1971).

The German youth movement came formally into existence at a meeting of the *Hohe Meissner* convocation in 1913, which gave rise to the Freideutsche Jugend (Free German Youth), an association of thirteen youth organizations some of which date back to the start of the twentieth century. That meeting represented an expression of revolt against adult society, particularly its authoritarianism, and a call for self-determination, opposition to conventional values of church, school and home, a striving for spiritual ideals, and an emphasis on experiencing nature (Burg,1998).

In a larger sense the rebellion against authority can be traced back more than a hundred years, to the period of

Sturm und Drang marked by the literary revolt against the repression of individual emotions and the creativity of youth. During this era, also, student groups attacked the symbols of Prussian autocracy and gave expression to some limited notions of democracy.

During the days of the Weimar Republic, the German youth movement reached a significant number of young people in the country. Over half the young males and a quarter of the young females were reported to be affiliated (Burg, 1998). The common goals outlined above do not hide the fact that there were substantial differences in emphasis among various youth movement organizations. While outright association with religious bodies and political parties was not the norm, youth groups represented disparate political orientations such as socialism, nationalism and anarchism. The National Socialist takeover of the German government led inevitably, albeit by stages, to the destruction of all independent youth organizations and their replacement by the Hitler Youth as a branch of the Nazi party.

For me, recruitment into the Jewish youth movement came at a particularly good time. Having been ousted in 1935 with all other Jewish students from the middle school, there was no alternative but to find a job. I was then fourteen years old and had completed eight grades the last four of which were in middle school. The local Jewish community had succeeded in setting up a structure for the education of children through the eighth grade, but there were no provisions for schooling beyond that level. My parents were in need of additional income after having been forced out of business by the Nazi boycott of Jewish stores. It thus became my responsibility to find work to supplement family income. Employment would have to be in an enterprise owned by Jews, because non-Jewish proprietors were no longer hiring "non-Aryans." My limited choice came down to an apprenticeship in business at a local cigar factory that was still in Jewish hands.

In the face of a job which held absolutely no interest for me and whose products I held in contempt (the *Werkleute* were strongly opposed to smoking), I found at that point that membership in the youth movement filled a big gap in my life. My hours of work extended from 7:30 AM to 3:30 PM. During the first year of my apprenticeship, I wrote addresses on shipping labels seven and a half hours a day. A more advanced assignment called for sorting out and stacking used cigar boxes for future use after reconditioning them in another department. What this involved escaped my attention, because I was not sufficiently interested in obtaining the relevant information.

The aforementioned assignments carried out day after day might have been a source of deep dissatisfaction were it not for the fact that this low-skilled work gave me an opportunity to let my mind roam and anticipate my role in the activities of the *Werkleute* group to which I belonged.

The *Werkleute* shared with the Weimar-era youth movements an emphasis on independence from adult (*bourgeois*) society and youth ritual, love of the outdoors, a romanticism that stressed a return to nature, and a rebellion against the formality and rigidity of the lives of the older generation. I must add, however, that rebellion against the parental home was not pronounced among the *Werkleute*, because the threats of the Nazi world created a measure of interdependence and solidarity between parents and children. Moreover, the salient characteristics of the movement such as identification with Judaism, Zionism, and political liberalism were shared in some measure by both generations.

The *Werkleute* differed from the Weimar German youth movement in a number of ways. Its membership was Jewish, which is hardly surprising since it came into being at a time when Jews were being excluded, step by step, from German life and German society. The dominant ideology of the *Werkleute* was Zionism, whose credo stressed the establishment of a Jewish state in Palestine (known as Israel after it came into being in 1948). Zionism has been defined in a number of ways depending on the type and degree of a person's involvement with the Jewish state. In the case of the *Werkleute* Zionism meant maximum involvement by abandoning life in the Diaspora and settling in a *Kibbutz* (collective settlement). For others the meaning of Zionism might express itself in merely believing in a homeland for the Jews or membership in a Zionist organization or contributing funds and services to the enterprise.

For teenagers like myself, Zionism had little meaning beyond personal belief, in view of the fact that parents usually make the decision on where minor children are going to be living. In the case of our *Werkleute* group, only a minority of members who survived settled in Jewish Palestine. Other destinations included the United States, South America, Australia, China, and wherever the family was able to negotiate a safe haven (a few families whose children were affiliated with the local chapter were unable to escape the Nazi hell). The seemingly higher survival rate among *Werkleute* families is the result of their having on the average more adequate financial resources that enabled them to buy their way out of the country. For us youngsters under eighteen who emigrated to a variety of places other than Palestine, the belief that settlement in Palestine is the only rational solution to the Jewish problem was unaffected by where our emigration took us. In short, we went where our parents made us go, often under protest.

The *Werkleute* movement's political orientation strongly favored the Labor Party or a coalition of labor and left-wing parties in the pre-state government of the *Yishuv* or Jewish settlement. The organization was also partial to the idea of a bi-national arrangement between Jews and Arabs in a future state. This orientation had the support of Judah Magnes, then president of the Hebrew University and Martin Buber, prominent philosopher and professor of Jewish philosophy at that institution. The bi-national state idea never became a political issue because there were no prominent Arabs who showed even the slightest interest in such a plan during the struggle for Palestinian independence.

The *Werkleute* viewed themselves as adherents of Martin Buber who affirmed a special affinity for the Zionist youth movement and their ideal of collective living while expressing reservations concerning their secularism. At the level of our younger youth groups we were cognizant of his writings on Hassidim (the 18th-century pietist movement), but his philosophic writings, some characterized by mysticism, were beyond our comprehension.

The movement's social philosophy tilted strongly in favor of socialism, a utopian form rooted in egalitarianism and humane values, as explicated by Buber. In the last years of the *Werkleute* movement this socialist orientation gave way to the Marxist kind whose realization was predicated on the class struggle. Two factors brought about the change—the bulk of its members (eighteen years and older who were able to leave Germany and go to Palestine) had settled in a *kibbutz* named Hazorea, which affiliated itself with the left-wing *kibbutz* movement known as Kibbutz Artzi. Kibbutz Artzi's ideology was unambiguously Marxist, and that association affected the political thinking of *Werkleute* members still left behind in Germany. They in turn joined forces with a Jewish youth organization in Germany, *Hashomer Hatzair* (the Young Guard), which was the youth branch of and feeder group for Kibbutz Artzi. A second likely reason for the German *Werkleute*'s adoption of a Marxist socialist philosophy was a greater identification with the Soviet Union whose Bolshevistic credo the Nazis branded as their greatest enemy. The feeling among many German Jews could be described by the saying "my enemy's enemy is my friend." This may fall short of a wholesale endorsement, but it must be remembered that the *Werkleute* were a group of young people eagerly searching for the ideal society characterized by social equality and freedom from capitalist domination. To the extent that the defects of the Soviet system were known, there was a tendency to deny them or view them as a reaction to the oppressive fascism spreading throughout Europe at that time.

For us fourteen- and fifteen-year-olds the *Werkleute*'s main attraction was peer group sociability. Social psychologists who were then studying the reasons why young people chose one movement or another that differed in their political or religious orientation found that choices were mainly made on the basis of friendship groupings rather than ideology. Ideology followed rather than preceded social attraction and compatibility.

Members of my group who were about fourteen years old and ranged in number from twelve to fifteen had several things in common: most of them lived in the same neighborhood of the city and had encountered each other in the past. All of them were at a developmental stage where planning for the future had become a serious consideration. They had been ousted or were in the process of being ousted from the German school system. The hastily arranged Jewish school programs available in the area did not extend beyond the eighth grade. The parents' plans for the family were contingent on opportunities to emigrate, and these varied from family to family depending on family connections abroad, financial resources, special parental skills that would lead to another country's invitation etc. For the teenagers in the *Werkleute,* this meant a state of suspension until the plans of their parents became clear.

In this planning vacuum, the youth movement played a crucial role. It had a plan for Jewish survival in Palestine. Its ideology commanded preparation for life in an emerging society, necessitating basic skills such as agriculture, home construction, water resource development, and manufacture of industrial products. Part of this ideology was the notion that a Jewish society in Palestine required that the roles of farmer and blue-collar worker would have to be filled by Jews if the new state were to constitute a normal society in contrast to the Diaspora where Jews were concentrated in business and the professions.

In keeping with this ideology, a few members of our group became apprentices in various manual trades while others enrolled in language courses or, as in my own case, secured employment that provided income on which families depended. In my case, it was necessary after my father was driven out of the shoe business. Learning a manual trade was, of course, completely in line with the idea of settling in a Palestinian Kibbutz. In actuality most of our group members had no control over their future because as teenagers they were dependent on the plans of their families. Nonetheless, learning a manual trade could also be viewed as potentially useful in the case of immigration to a country other than Palestine, where the possession of manual skills would facilitate employment for those who were not yet fluent in the local language.

For most of us belonging to the *Werkleute,* it sustained us socially and ideologically, and the dissonance between ideals and actual plans for immigration did not burden us, rationalizing as we did that sooner or later we would end up living in a Palestinian Kibbutz, which we considered the only rational solution to the Jewish problem.

The Mannheim branch of the *Werkleute* offered a myriad of activities which included Onegey Shabbat (welcoming the sabbath meetings), Saturday afternoon discussion groups, Sunday hikes, camping trips, and informal get-togethers with one or more group members at least three times a week. The group had voted for such an arrangement suggested by the group leader, Eric Boehm, and most of us adhered to it.

In common with the basic credo of behavior shared with the youth movements of the Weimar Republic, the *Werkleute* disapproved of smoking and drinking alcohol, condemned conspicuous consumption, and advocated a simple dress code that comprised shirts, blouses, sweaters, skirts, and short pants for boys. For festive occasions, white shirts were worn.

Within the context of the basic movement values outlined above, the group presented a wealth of cultural offerings. In retrospect, it appears to me that they more than made up for the schooling I missed as a result of the Nazis' aryanization of education. Some of the offerings were bolstered by cultural programs such as concerts, library services, language classes sponsored by the Jewish community at little or no cost to the consumer (Mannheim had an extraordinary amount of Jewish talent and was known as one of the prime centers of German Jewish life).

In my *Werkleute* group, singing was a core activity. We all had a large repertory of songs, mostly in German and Hebrew, but some also in Yiddish, French, and English. The songs were drawn from Jewish and Zionist history, Jewish liturgy, life in Palestine, revolutionary wars of various countries, and the Weimar youth movement (hiking songs, rounds, and songs dealing with nature). We all knew them by heart. We avoided song sheets, because they would have provided evidence to Nazi investigators of the dissident nature of our activities.

Most meetings began with singing, and the choice of songs was not random but attuned to the subject of the meeting. One group member would start a song and the rest would instantly join in. From time to time, someone, usually Eric, the group leader, would teach us a new tune that would be added to our repertoire.

The weekly Saturday afternoon meetings were devoted to discussion of some subject of interest prepared by Eric. Occasionally, we had a guest discussion leader, and over time group members would take a turn at making the presentation. Most meetings were held by our group alone, composed only of boys, but from time to time we held joint meetings or outings with the girls' group our age or jointly with the membership of the whole local chapter. A few members of our group had talent for composing and presenting skits which attracted outsiders, a source of special pride for us.

The ethos of the group put a premium on team effort and achievement rather than individual attainment. This found its clearest expression in sports contests (mini-Olympiads) in which the total group was divided into small teams that were carefully balanced relative to individual athletic ability in various sports. The teams not only practiced together but developed posters, songs, cheers, and other morale-building techniques.

Periodically, the group held sessions devoted to critiquing its work and the behavior of its members. This was done in the spirit of self-criticism rather than pointing the finger at others. Participants in the sessions discussed their own problems and encouraged fellow members in their quest to remedy or cope with them. There was a remarkable absence of hostility or bitterness (or at least the expression of such), largely due to Eric's skillful manner of guiding the discussion. He would call together the group two or three times a year for a critiquing session, held in a festive candle-light ceremony in the course of which a group member would be given a *Kordel* or braided cord as a recognition for contributions made to the work of the group.

Joint events with the girls' group, which became more frequent as we got older, included chamber musicals (several of us played the recorder, a few the piano), holiday commemorations, and walks and bicycle trips. Interest in the opposite sex was limited to a few and dating activities to joint walks or bicycle trips, but "going steady" was frowned upon. My most vivid recollection from an outing with the girls' group is our challenging them to a game of Voelkerball (which resembles volleyball) rather than inviting mixed teams and receiving a humiliating beating from the "weaker" sex.

During the period preceding *Kristallnacht* (November 9,1938), Jewish life became increasingly unsettled in Germany. The Nuremberg Laws passed in September 1935 had disenfranchised the German Jews and made them non-citizens. This meant they were unable to hold government jobs, vote in elections, marry non-Jews, or hire non-Jewish domestic workers. Pressure on Germans not to patronize Jewish businesses or accept their professional services became the order of the day. In 1938, Jewish-owned industrial enterprises were forced to close or "aryanize," meaning accept non-Jewish ownership.

A few members of the older *Werkleute* group, about five years our senior, were making preparations to go to Palestine. Some members of my own group had parents who were busy with arrangements for emigration. If their children were informed about the nature of these arrangements, they tended not to share it with their peers. The reasons were obvious. The parental plans ran counter to movement ideology, which acknowledged only one solution to the miseries of Diaspora living: life in Palestine. We realized, of course, that millions of Jews led a benign existence in countries such as the United States, England, Australia, Scandinavia, but their future, the argument went, could only be assured in a Jewish homeland.

The parents had their own reasons for not publicizing their impending plans to leave. There was constant fear that had both rational and irrational foundations, fear that knowledge of the plans could create obstacles to their realization. Some schemes for escaping the Nazi hell involved the paying of bribes; others frontier crossing without a permit. Being accused of violating the stringent currency laws was another justified fear.

Within the group yet another reason existed for departing quickly and silently. Those lucky enough to have found a way to freedom saw little reason to display their good fortune before friends who were left behind. In point of fact, I do not recall a single farewell party for my friends who left Germany during the years of the Nazi regime. To this day, I am unable to account for either the exact time or precise destination of their departure.

So during 1937 an increasing number of families of my *Werkleute* group left for places as diverse a England, the United States, China, and Palestine. Among those leaving for the United States was Eric, our group leader. His departure was a major loss to me because he had been my role model since the time I joined the *Werkleute*. His successor, Kurt Reilinger, was a likable person with a good sense of humor, but he led the group for less than a year. At that point, membership had shrunk to half a dozen as a result of accelerated emigration.

Also contributing to the rapid decline of the Mannheim *Werkleute* was the untimely and tragic death of Louise Bauer, beloved leader of the girls' group and sister of the national head of the *Werkleute*. This was the first confrontation for any of us with the death of a young friend, and we emerged badly shaken, finding it difficult to cope with the event. Weeks passed before we were able to get together and commemorate Louise's life, which we had so greatly admired.

From mid-1937 to the fall of 1938 membership in the

local chapter dwindled. The social and cultural activities in our group proceeded at a low ebb as families and children became more preoccupied with ways of fleeing Nazi Germany. By the beginning of 1938, our group had dwindled to three and we joined forces with the remnants of a group, slightly older, of *Hashomer Hatzair* (the Young Guard). This was an international Labor Zionist organization with a socialist orientation. As stated above, *Hashomer Hatzair* was the youth movement affiliate of Kibbutz Artzi, a Kibbutz movement with which the adult *Werkleute*, already settled in Israel, had affiliated. They did so after they set up their own agricultural settlement named *Hazorea*.

Our combined Mannheim group numbered no more than eight or ten, but it was now composed of boys and girls. We formed close ties and enjoyed outings and overnight trips and joint cultural activities. But it seemed clear to us that this was all very temporary, that in a matter of months we would be leaving the scene in any feasible manner for destinations that would include Palestine, the United States, England, and some other European countries.

During an interim period of six months I accepted the task of taking on the leadership of a preteen boys group, but the project failed largely because the children were leaving Germany with their parents at too rapid a rate to keep the youth group going.

At home our family life became subject to incredible stresses. In the spring of 1937 I was dismissed from my job because the firm I had worked for was aryanized or turned over to non-Jewish owners. That meant the loss of a salary, however small, that contributed to the financial upkeep of my family. Following the closing of my parents' shoestore, my mother had become the main wage earner, teaching dressmaking to Jewish women who were preparing to leave Germany. These were middle-class women, some with college degrees, who were counting on their newly acquired manual skills to serve as a source of support in countries whose language they did not know.

Sometime early in 1936, my brother Siegbert left for Spain, in response to an invitation from our uncle, my mother's only brother, to join him and his wife in Barcelona. During his stay, the Spanish Civil War broke out and quickly engulfed much of the country. I recall several of Siegbert's letters describing with enthusiasm the defeat of the Franco mutiny in Barcelona at the hands of the Loyalist army composed of security forces and armed workers in the early days of the war.

In the summer of 1937, with the civil war spreading throughout the north my brother left Spain to return home. My family had no warning that this was about to happen, and there had been no consultation between my uncle and my family on Siegbert's impending move. Our first realization of what was happening took the form of a notification by the German authorities that he had been arrested at the French border and was being held in prison.

My father was allowed to visit him briefly and under close supervision, which left no room for exchanging information. My father was left with the impression that my brother had planned to visit us before going to the United States (we had no idea whether he had made preparations for such a move). If true this would indicate enormous naïvité on his part and perhaps that of my uncle as well regarding the status of Jews under the Hitler regime. It is possible that the German authorities had a dossier on Siegbert, based on intercepted letters. On the other hand, arbitrary arrests of Jews and other enemies of the state were routine and required no explanation. A few weeks after Siegbert's imprisonment in a civilian jail, he was transferred to Dachau, the first large concentration camp set up by the S.S. in the Munich area, to deal with dissident elements in the German population (of an estimated 40,000 dissidents who were murdered at Dachau 80 to 90 percent were Jews). We saw this as a most ominous development but did not give up hope since stories circulated of people having been released from Dachau. We did not know of any such cases and were unable to have any story of release confirmed, still hoped for the best.

Our worst fears came true on the fifth of August, 1937, when a representative of the Gestapo (the Nazi secret police) came to our home and informed us that Siegbert had died as a result of suicide. He carried with him my brother's overcoat, a watch, and some coins of German currency, for all of which we had to sign a receipt, presumably as a testimony to the Nazis' honesty. My parents were given permission to attend the funeral performed by a Munich rabbi, but the coffin was not to be opened.

As a 1945 postscipt to this family tragedy I can furnish further information on the death of Siegbert. Shortly after the conquest of Munich I went to Dachau as a member of the American military government and demanded access to information about my brother. The caretakers of the camp records, most of them displaced persons, showed me an index card which noted three confinements to the Bunker, an isolation chamber for solitary confinement or special punishment. A cross followed the date of the third confinement. Bunkers are not places where people commit suicide. Rather they are venues for torture and murder.

Personally, by sheer luck, I was spared punitive confinement by the authorities except for one occasion of arrest and detention during a round-up of organizers of Jewish youth groups by uniformed brown-shirts. A gang with no identification picked me up at work and forced me into their automobile. They asked me whether I knew how to swim as they were planning to throw me off the Rhein bridge. I assured them that I was an experienced swimmer, and that ended the conversation. Their first stop was at my home where, without explanation to my parents, they began ransacking closets in search for forbidden materials. In my bedroom wardrobe they found a copy of Kurt Tucholsky's *Das Laecheln der Monalisa* (The *Smile of the Mona Lisa*), a book lent to me by a friend which I had hidden in the closet, because I knew it was on the banned books list (that was not very smart of me, and I realized my mistake when the brown-shirts entered my house).

Tucholsky was a well-known essayist and social critic with a left orientation, during the years of the Weimar Republic. Fortunately, my investigators had not done their homework, and their attention was quickly diverted to a book dealing with sex education of children which they confiscated. I was transported to a downtown party office where they held other Jewish group leaders. Several hours later, they released all of us with a warning that our activities were being watched. I lost no time phoning my parents with the good news and an urgent request to destroy the banned book lest we have another visit from more sophisticated investigators. The reason for the round-up escapes me in view of the fact that a tightly controlled society such as Nazi Germany left no room and opportunity for anti-state activity. Moreover, a system like the Nazi government, which writes its own laws that are arbitrary by international standards, does not need to justify itself in order to engage in cruel conduct. More likely, the brown-shirts' activity was an instance of terror for the sake of terror or a rehearsal for more significant interventions in the future.

A decisive turning point in the treatment of Jews occurred on November 9, 1938, in the form of an event that came to be known as the *Kristallnacht* or night of the broken glass. At the beginning of the month the counselor Ernst vom Rath at the German embassy in Paris was assassinated by Herschel Grynszpan who declared that he avenged the injustices done by the Nazis to his parents. Under the pretext of retaliation the Nazis, on the night of November 9, set fire to 191 German synagogues, arrested more than 30,000 Jews and sent them to concentration camps. They looted also thousands of Jewish homes, stores, and shops, and imposed a fine of one billion marks on all German Jewry. An undisclosed number of the arrested died as a result of harsh treatment meted out at the camps and exposure to the wintry conditions.

The main synagogue in Mannheim was torched and completely gutted. Not one of the homes of our relatives and Jewish friends escaped being invaded by groups of brown-shirts, although the amount of theft and vandalism varied. Male adults of any age were arrested and promptly transported to Dachau.

On the morning of November 10, I left for work early at a mittens factory owned by a distant relative who had provided me with temporary employment after I was discharged from the cigar factory, now in non-Jewish hands.

The mittens factory, a relatively small enterprise employing no more than six or eight people, was also in the process of a forced takeover. The prospective non-Jewish owner shared information with us, not yet public knowledge, about the anti-Jewish raid and pogrom that was being launched about the time I arrived at work. He told me to get on my bicycle and keep riding non-stop until nightfall when the action would end, so as to escape capture.

I did what I was told to do. However, for reasons not entirely clear to me, I decided to ride past my home, a fourth floor apartment in Mannheim's inner city. A crowd had gathered in front of the entrance, watching a bonfire that was being fed by books being thrown out of our apartment windows. Although nobody among those gathered appeared to recognize me, I decided not to take a chance and continued riding my bike. A quick glance at the crowd revealed a small group of activists, mostly young, some in Hitler Youth uniform, who tended the fire and a larger group of bystanders who looked with embarrassment at the flames.

After continuing my ride until sundown, avoiding areas where the anti-Jewish rampage was in progress, I returned home. The crowd had vanished, and the evidence of the bonfire had been removed. From my mother and sister Hedy I learned that at midmorning a group of Nazis, some in uniform, forced their way into the apartment and arrested my father. They had my name at the head of the list of those to be taken into custody, but when told that I was at work did not pursue the matter further. The gang went through drawers and closets, looking for moncy, jewelry, and other valuables. They then set to work removing all the books from the cabinets and shelves and heaving them out of the apartment windows.

The search for valuables yielded only one gold bracelet. The leader of the gang handed it to a teenager in the group, presumably a member of the Hitler Youth, and asked him to hold on to it. My mother and my sister watched as the boy moments later returned the bracelet to the drawer from which it had been lifted. There was a moment of high drama in this act, for it was not unlikely that the group leader would demand the return of the bracelet and hold either the boy or, worse yet, my mother responsible for its absence.

Seconds before the raid began my mother had the foresight to hide all the cash in the house in a cloth sack on top of the gas meter located in the toilet. The leader of the raiding party had requested all money and other valuables the moment they entered our home. My mother had ignored the request. Had they found the cash we would have been left without any monetary resources, because like many other Jewish families we shied away from German banks whose management of Jewish funds was controlled by the Nazi government. The hidden money included a sum my parents had put aside for my voyage to the United States.

Following the search of our home, the gang descended to a second-floor apartment where another Jewish family lived. The man of the house was not at home, because a non-Jewish neighbor across the hall, who was also the building's landlord, had given him shelter. Here within the space of perhaps half an hour we witnessed two instances of courageous non-compliance in a society where terror was a hallmark of daily existence.

On the same evening my mother went on a mission to determine my father's whereabouts. First she went to the local police headquarters from where she was sent to the main office of the Gestapo, the Nazi secret police. The destination sounded ominous. Internment in Dachau where my brother lost his life a year earlier was too dreadful a thought to contemplate. True to form, the Gestapo declined to give her any information, but within a day or so word was out that all Jewish males arrested on November 10 were on their way to Dachau.

The overriding issue in emigration as a viable option was the lack of opportunities for resettlement. The borders of other countries were either closed or open for only a trickle of certain kinds of immigrants—first-degree relatives of one of their citizens or persons highly skilled in specific fields. A conference on the German refugee problem, convened in July 1937 at Evian by U.S. President Franklin D. Roosevelt, yielded only negligible results. The Jewish exodus from Germany during the Nazi regime depended also on people's financial resources, preferably in a foreign country. Having cash to pay for visas, travel, first accommodations, etc. was an absolute necessity. Even emigration to Palestine, the choice of the most committed Zionists, required payment of 1,000 British Pounds for a visa. Palestine was administered by Great Britain under a League of Nations mandate. There did exist a few exceptions to this expensive and bureaucratic process of emigration such as Youth *Aliyah* (or Jewishly organized immigration of young Jews to Palestine) and the children's transport to England, involving 10,000 boys and girls in December 1938.

While the quest for leaving Germany represented until 1938 an ever widening and intensified search for "a way out," it became a mass panic after *Kristallnacht* as German Jews came to realize that the Nazis were hell-bent on eliminating them from the German population (at the end of 1938 about 164,000 out of the pre-Nazi Jewish population of 500,000 had emigrated from Germany (Bauer, Y., p.109).

German Jews, in desperation, pursued every avenue of exit known to them, even to underdeveloped nations and countries in the orbit of potential Nazi aggression such as France, Holland, Belgium, Denmark, and Norway, to escape the most immediate threat to their existence. Visa applications flooded the United States consulates, resulting in long waiting lists which, in the light of the menacing political developments, left little hope for the bulk of the applicants. At the start of the war, only about one half of the Jews of Germany and Austria had succeeded in emigrating (Bauer, p.109).

My own family, already caught up in the events surrounding *Kristallnacht* as a result of my father's arrest and internment in Dachau, was searching for a quick escape. My mother sent two telegrams to her brother and his wife, who were longtime residents and citizens of Spain. We felt that even Spain, embroiled in a vicious civil war, would be preferable to being trapped in the Nazi purgatory. The telegrams went unanswered, but after a delay of more than a week produced a response in the form of a letter expressing regret over being unable to help us (my uncle was a well-established business man living in Barcelona, while his wife was a painter and sculptor who had received public recognition for her work).

My mother had asserted all along—long before *Kristallnacht*—that despite her prediction that the Jews will survive the Hitler regime, she wanted us children to leave the country as quickly as possible. Hence my parents' decision to send my brother to Spain, a well-intentioned move whose tragic outcome was beyond their control. They had also made an application before *Kristallnacht* on my behalf for a visa to the United States. No provisions had yet been made for my sister Hedy who, as the youngest at age fourteen, was thought to be joining my parents when the opportunity arose for refuge in Spain.

Hedy's chance to leave the country arose suddenly and quite unexpectedly in December 1938 when the British cabinet, in response to the Nazi November riots, decided to allow 10,000 Jewish children from Germany, Austria and Czechoslovakia to enter England, putting their maintenance into the hands of refugee organizations. Among my mother's students in the dressmaking course she taught was the head of the Mannheim Jewish welfare service, Mia Neter, who administered the local children's transport program. When Mrs. Neter asked my mother whether she would like Hedy to be included in the program the answer was an instantaneous and decisive yes. A couple of days later, my sister was on her way. I was charged with the responsibility of bidding her farewell at the local train station since my father was interned in Dachau and my mother felt it was her duty to remain with the dressmaking students at that hour.

The children traveled in groups, accompanied by a few adults who looked after them up to the point where British personnel took over from them at the border crossing. The Jewish families had only the vaguest ideas about the children's future whereabouts and conditions of living, but they surely must have shared my mother's point of view that almost any arrangement out of reach of the German authorities would be a big gain for the children.

My father returned home from Dachau after my sister's departure but prior to my leaving for the United States in March 1939. He said very little about his experiences at the concentration camp, having been intimidated by threats of rearrest if word were to get out about life at Dachau. He thought he was released earlier than many others because he had been a frontline soldier in World War I, but he expressed no hope that his status would earn him special considerations in the future. With help from friends, my parents obtained an affidavit of support from a New York businessman, a first step in the long process of securing a visa to the United States. The length of the waiting list for the German immigration quota left no room for optimism about a timely rescue. In the meantime, all efforts were devoted to getting me out of the country.

At the beginning of 1939, the Zionist youth movement in Mannheim had shrunk to a fraction of its original membership. The remaining *Werkleute* members combined with the remnants of *Hashomer Hatzair* (The Young Guard) which was more decidedly Marxist. Ideological differences were no longer an issue. Our concern was with a safe way to leave the country. Some members of our group, which at that point numbered fewer than ten, were giving some thought to crossing the border illegally. Others were waiting for the issuance of immigration papers in process. We got together often, mostly on weekends, since we were engaged in a variety of activities, some community related, during the rest of the week. Overnight camping was a favorite morale builder. When we talked about the future we envisioned meeting again in Palestine in a Kibbutz without a clear idea on how to get from here to there.

My own job ended in December 1938, when the mittens factory was transferred to non-Jewish ownership. With my departure to the United States scheduled for the middle of March, my mother advised against looking for another job. Jobs for Jews had become scarce since the general labor market was closed to them.

The trip from my home to Hamburg, the port of embarkation, had threatening moments of its own. I shared a train compartment with several men, including three brown-shirts, who were drinking beer. At some point, perhaps under the influence of the alcohol, they started to throw the empty beer bottles out of the window of the moving train. At the next train stop a railroad official entered to investigate who was responsible for the bottle tossing, which supposedly had barely missed the head of a pedestrian walking near the train. There was silence. I had good reason to fear that somebody would blame me, because as a Jew I was the most natural victim. However, during the course of the trip the men had paid no attention to me and knew nothing about my identity. The train official may also have dropped the matter in view of the fact that nobody was injured and the seeming inebriated behavior pointed to the brown-shirts as the guilty party.

This incident brought to my mind a previous occasion when I had to act hastily to avoid being victimized according to the Nazi interpretation of a situation. Walking in front of the railroad station a girl, approximately my age, riding a bicycle ran into me—or I might have run into her—and fell off the bike. I shouted "Sorry," and walked away, being well aware of the consequences of a Jew becoming entangled with an "Aryan" citizen. Seconds later a man picked the woman off the ground and called me a boor for not assisting her when she was in trouble. From his vantage point he was right, and I felt very badly about not having helped the woman. Here is, indeed, an example of how in the pre-holocaust period of Nazi rule the relationships between Jews and non-Jews had already been structured in such a manner as to keep the Jew constantly on his or her guard.

When I arrived at the harbor on March 15, a more ominous threat was posed by the news that Germany had invaded Czechoslovakia and was in the process of annexing it. A rumor was spreading among those awaiting embarkation on the S.S. *Roosevelt* that we would not be allowed to leave. Fortunately the rumor was found to be untrue, and we sailed as planned.

Early on the following morning the ship encountered extremely heavy seas. The desk officer described them as rougher than any he had seen in his many years of service. My personal feeling was one of great relief, for I believed that no storm could equal the dangers and miseries of life in Nazi Germany. There was only the gnawing feeling of distress over the fact that my parents were left behind.

2

Confusing Signals in a Free Society

In a message to the Booksellers of America in 1942, President Franklin D. Roosevelt of the United States wrote these words: "We all know that books burn—yet we have the greater knowledge that books cannot be killed by fire." This statement still represents to me a most striking contrast between Nazi Germany that had provided me with a personal version of book burning and the United States, which offered me shelter in March, 1939.

The voyage to the United States, except for the stormy first hours at sea, was uneventful. By chance, I encountered a small number of people from my hometown, Mannheim. The amount of food served on the ship, the S.S. *Roosevelt*, was awesome, and the quality exceeded any food experience I recalled in my eighteen years of life. I watched in shock and amazement as tons of food were tossed overboard at the end of the day.

One group of passengers I encountered on the trip held a special fascination for me. They were members of the former Lincoln Brigade, American volunteers in the army of the Spanish loyalists who had resisted the Franco uprising and eventual overthrow of the Spanish republic. These young people were very guarded in their conversation for reasons I did not understand till much later. My limited knowledge of English also hampered my communication.

The group's appeal resided in their idealism and their resolve to combat the spread of Spanish, German and other brands of fascism at a time when most of the worlds' nations found themselves unable to react. While living in Germany we found ourselves cut off from any flow of information about events in Spain, and what we knew was part of the lore of socialist youth movement, stories and songs brought by an occasional foreign visitor.

When I approached one of the returnees from Spain with a request to teach me some of the songs of the International Brigade, he sat me down and said in a fatherly manner that I should wait until I am settled in the United States and received my citizenship papers. The meaning and likely wisdom of his advice largely escaped me at that point.

At the time of arrival my knowledge of American history and politics was sketchy, to say the least, but I had heard of the Statue of Liberty which the ship passed in the early twilight on the way to its berth in Manhattan. Though busy with preparations for landing (packing and filling out forms), I was quickly swept up by the sense of excitement as everyone rushed on deck for a glimpse of the colossal lady, the enduring symbol of welcome to those "yearning to breathe free."

New York was not to be my final American destination for three reasons: 1. My sponsor, a cousin of my mother known as Linchen (she had provided me with an affidavit for immigration), had made as a condition of sponsorship that I not settle anywhere near her (no one asked for an explanation, but she probably feared financial dependency). 2. My uncle Solomon, my father's elder brother and his second wife Helene (his first wife had succumbed to heart disease), had invited me to stay with them in their home in Saint Paul, Minnesota. 3. Furthermore, given the choice between living in the megalopolis and a medium-sized city, I much preferred the latter. Intuition rather than experience guided me in my preference, which may also have been influenced by the fact that I had grown up in a city of comparable size to Saint Paul. Life in a midwestern city turned out to be a good choice despite a somewhat bumpy start. Linchen, I was told, showed little interest in my progress in the new country. Some twenty-five years later, after I had acquired a family and a secure academic position in the New York area, she declined my offer of a courtesy visit.

Linchen's experience as a young German immigrant to the United States had taught her to be self-sufficient and perhaps she had every right to expect me to fend for myself. She arrived in New York and landed a job as secretary for a well-established physician. Her holdings listed on the sponsorship papers contained AT&T stock in excess of $100,000, a substantial sum in the late 1930s. Sponsoring my immigration was not something that came to her naturally. In fact another of my mother's cousins, Julius Baumann, a recent immigrant from Mannheim, had found it necessary to stage a sit-in at Linchen's office before she agreed to prepare an affidavit for me.

Prior to my departure for Minnesota she granted me a brief "interview" in front of her office. She expressed her pleasure at my having made arrangements to leave New York and gave me a parting gift of fifteen dollars which was almost enough for a one-way bus ticket to Saint Paul.

With the money left over from exchanging German marks into dollars (ten dollars was the maximum allowed per person) I still retained three dollars to be used for food and other necessities on the trip. I departed New York with the good feeling that I was free of debt and did not have a worry in the world.

Two weeks in New York City—staying first with the Julius Baumann family, then with the family of Eric Boehm, my former *Werkleute* group leader—were a dazzling experience. At five cents a subway ride and with good shoeleather protecting my feet (my father had been a shoe salesman) I was able to take in most of the tourist sights . But after ten days of touring I decided, like many visitors, that New York City is a great place to visit but not to inhabit.

These sentiments were reinforced after I took my place on the New York–Chicago Greyhound bus late at night. I fell asleep as the bus entered the Lincoln Tunnel and awoke some miles beyond as we rode through suburban New Jersey areas. After two weeks in a concrete jungle, as I was now surrounded by small houses, gardens, an occasional park, and river crossings, a feeling of calm and peace of mind flooded my consciousness.

Traveling on a Greyhound bus to me was a journey in luxury. It certainly was that compared to riding on the hard benches in third class compartments of the German Reichsbahn. But it was also my first opportunity to become acquainted with small-town America as the bus made stops along the way to pick up and discharge passengers. For a single passenger like myself, the turnover in riders provided a chance to become engaged in conversation. The periodic rest stops allowed for a mingling with townspeople who were on duty in cafeterias and tourist shops and quite eager to chat when business was slow, particularly on the night shift. My fractured English, rather than alienating people, had the effect of inviting questions about my origin and destination and also brought forth ready advice when I asked for it.

Upon arrival in Saint Paul I discovered quickly that the name of the game would be living within a set structure of rules of behavior in the household of my aunt Helene. The other residents, my uncle Sol and two young boys, children of Helene's brother and sister-in-law, who were waiting for visas to the United States. A sixth resident of the household, an upper duplex apartment, was also a German-Jewish immigrant and employed as an insurance agent, who rented a bedroom in the flat.

Helene was the second wife of my uncle Sol, a widower, whose first wife had succumbed to heart disease. He entered into the second marriage with a woman, perhaps twelve to fifteen years younger than himself who had never been married before and had had a successful professional career. The marriage was arranged by relatives of the couple and had as one of its goals joint emigration to the United States.

Helene had a cousin, Henry Weiller, who lived in Saint Paul, Minnesota and owned a lucrative cattle business that was part of the Saint Paul stockyards, then second in size only to the Chicago yards of Carl Sandburg fame. Henry, a native of Switzerland, who had come to the United States as a boy, had acted as a sponsor for the immigration to the United States of all his relatives, a group of cousins living in Germany. Among these cousins was my aunt Helene.

I had met Helene only briefly before she and Sol left for the United States. My parents were only superficially acquainted with her, but following Helene's invitation to have me join them in Saint Paul, we all agreed that living there would be a good alternative to settling in New York City.

Henry found a job for Sol in his stockyards just as he had made arrangements for employment for the other cousins. When Sol arrived in Minnesota he was sixty years old. It will be recalled that in Mannheim he had been the owner of a fairly profitable store and, with the exception of service in the infantry during World War I, had never performed physical labor in his life. Herding cattle in the Minnesota climate known for its cold winters and hot humid summers, would have been a tough assignment for anyone. For Sol, a short, skinny, late middle-aged man, it was an astonishing feat. I never heard him complain in the least about the difficulties inherent in the job.

His wife, Helene, as the head of the six-person household, ran a tight ship. The two-bedroom flat was fully utilized spacially, with one bedroom being used by my uncle and aunt and the other given over to a roomer. Two nephews of Helene slept in a sunroom off the living room, and I occupied an alcove connected to the living-dining room.

The rules of the house were made clear by Helene shortly after my arrival. My rental for room and board would be $7.00 per week, with credit extended until I found a job (my inquiries indicated that this amount was on the high side at that time). Lights would be turned off at nine PM. If I had to take lunch to work two sandwiches would be the limit (at the time of my arrival in the States I was considerably underweight). When I failed to extinguish the lights precisely at nine o'clock in my doorless room, my meek and patient uncle was dispatched to enforce the law.

I don't recall being terribly upset over the regimentation in my aunt's house. Although my mother had no clue about Helene's proclivities, she prepared me for possible hard times in a new country whose conditions I was not familiar with. As for myself, I discovered in no time that the grass was greener almost anywhere outside my aunt's house, and I arranged my day accordingly.

To fill the time until I found a job, a volunteer worker of the Saint Paul Jewish Family Service arranged for me to attend high school day classes to learn English. With the influx of Jewish immigrants who had fled Nazi Germany, the JFS had set up a program to help the newcomers become adjusted to life in this midwestern city.

My first paid job was employment on weekends in a downtown grocery store, sorting strawberries and moving other fruits and vegetables from a storeroom to the sales counters of the store. After a relatively short time a series of full-time jobs materialized, generally of a temporary or seasonal nature, requiring no particular skills or knowledge of the English language. Whenever a job ended, I got myself a list of businesses, mostly under Jewish ownership, and made the rounds until somebody agreed to hire me. I had the impression that the relative ease with which I was able to find employment was at least in part due to the fact that the owners of the businesses were motivated to assist Jewish refugees like myself find a place in American society. This at least was my supposition after being asked by fellow students at night high school, which I attended after finding work during the day, how I was able to land a job while they had been unsuccessful in their search for employment.

Nonetheless, the kind of employment I experienced provided a minimum of job security and no fringe benefits other than money put aside for social security. Notice of a forthcoming lay-off were usually given on the last day of work.

Among the remarkable people with whom I became associated in Saint Paul and who contributed greatly to my integration into American society was Mollie Weiller, wife of Henry Weiller. Henry, as noted above, can rightly be credited with the survival of his German relatives, among them my aunt Helene, whose immigration to the United States he had sponsored.

Mollie Weiller's home had become a social center for Jewish immigrants like myself who had settled in Saint Paul, Minnesota.

She organized periodic social gatherings at her house and outings and always saw to it that her parties brought together a mix of newcomers and longtime residents who could serve as role models for the recent arrivals.

Mollie had lost her sight a few years earlier after extended efforts by medical practitioners to keep her from going blind. I am uncertain about the cause, but it may have been macular degeneration. From the moment I met her, I never ceased being amazed at her ability to navigate through life successfully, given the fact that her handicap originated in midlife. In her presence one was hardly aware of her affliction, given the way in which she organized her home, carried on an active correspondence (using a typewriter), participated in organizations as a member as well as officer (she served at one point as local president of Hadassah, the women's Zionist Organization), wrote playlets, entertained guests and did all the other things that "normal" people are expected to do.

Mollie's frequent invitations, often for dinner, created for me a home away from home. Reading aloud to her was an activity that was important to both of us. My learning of English was helped enormously by her correcting my pronunciation. For Mollie this was an opportunity to gain access to literature that was not available in the library of Talking Books (Recordings for the Blind) whose inventory in the late 1930s was limited. Our mutual enjoyment in joint reading was anchored in the fact that we shared similar interests. We were both Zionists (Mollie was an active member of Hadassah). Our political views were definitely left of center (she was a member of the Women's International League for Peace and Freedom). We enjoyed reading Lincoln Steffens, Dos Passos, Pierre Van Paassen. Novels we read included Shalom Asch's *Three Cities* and Richard Wright's *Native Son.*

Within four months after my arrival in Saint Paul I landed my first full-time job at Stuart Products, a factory making perfume novelties, mainly for the Christmas season. The business had a small core staff year round and hired in August and September a staff of several dozens, mainly women, who assembled the novelties that encased a small bottle of inexpensive perfume. One of my tasks required siphoning this perfume from five gallon containers into the small novelty bottles, a process that called for a quick shift of the hose from the mouth to the bottles. In beginning the siphoning process, care had to be taken to avoid the onset of the flow going into the mouth rather than into the novelties. An occasional failure to do so resulted in an unwelcome swallow of perfume and/or a drenching of clothing with the perfume whose odor did not endear me to my fellow passengers in the streetcar on the way home.

There were two men besides myself, Jim and Russel, doing the siphoning and all the other heavier physical work. We became friends quickly and enjoyed occasional after-hours sociability including a weekend fishing trip to northern Minnesota. My job, night school classes, frequent visits to the Weiller home, and sports (tennis, swimming, and skating in the winter) provided me with a schedule of activities, which were reasonably satisfying and limited my stay at aunt Helene's house to the late night and early morning hours.

I never mentioned my distaste for living at Helene's house to Mollie nor did she ever ask any questions about my stay there. I was, therefore, immensely surprised and pleased at the same time when she asked me whether I would be interested to live with them. The Weillers had an adopted son, David, who suffered from epilepsy and lived at home only periodically. When there he argued frequently with his parents who had little influence on him although he was financially dependent on them. Because of his illness, which at that time could not be controlled by drugs, David was unable to hold a job. Employment in Henry's business was tried but did not work out. I had a superficial relationship with David, but when he lived at home, I did not feel any resentment directed toward me.

Mollie's instructions to me were as follows: "Just take from your place as much as you can carry. I shall inform Helene of the change." I insisted on paying for room and board, an arrangement which Mollie at first rejected but accepted with a much smaller amount than I had offered, presumably to appease my pride. Helene and Sol kept their distance from the Weillers for some weeks but eventually decided not to hold a grudge against their benefactors who, after all, had sponsored their coming to the United States.

At night high school which I attended after landing a daytime job, I took courses in English literature (Beowulf, Chaucer, Milton) and speech. My prior formal education comprised eight grades, four of which were elementary schooling followed by four years of middle school. The German system at that time was split into two tracks: the elementary one which covered eight grades of mandatory schooling and the middle school track, which, by contrast, contained a maximum of nine grades organized into different streams, depending on one's prospective choice of academic or business career. My own schooling had ended with the fourth grade of middle school (*Oberrealschule*). This was an ending in nowhere and a forced accommodation to the expulsion of Jews from the public school system.

I registered for the high school courses with the primary goal of improving my English but also the thought in back of my mind that it might eventually lead to a high school degree. At the time I reached the United States a college education was unthinkable. After all, I had come to America to help my parents and contribute to their support. Moreover, neither my family background (lower middle-class) nor my ideological peer group environment (preparation for life in a Palestinian Kibbutz) left any room for an academic education. Plans for Kibbutz living had by now been pushed into the more distant future, given the uncertainties posed by a spreading war that threatened to engulf much of the world.

What happened next put me into an upbeat state of turmoil. The principal of the night high school (Mechanic Arts) came in at the end of one of the class sessions and said to me that I was wasting my time. I did not understand the meaning of this, but did not feel that I could challenge his authority. I personally felt that I was learning something and beyond that enjoyed the classes. Following that statement he handed me a letter addressed to the University of Minnesota Testing Service. That same respect for authority led me to go to the Testing Service and accept their invitation to participate in a program of psychometric and knowledge testing. I had never heard of such tests, let alone taken one. Even now, some sixty years later, I am not sure whether asking me to take the tests was designed as an offer, based on the judgment of my teachers, to accelerate my education or an invitation to serve as a guinea pig in an educational experiment. Could it be that both reasons applied?

After a week's testing of some four to five hours each day, with a break for lunch, I was accepted as an undergraduate student at the University of Minnesota on probation with the proviso that I maintain at least a "B" average. I couldn't believe my good fortune. From a youngster without educational credentials (I had destroyed my German report cards together with my passport marked with a "J" for Jude) because I thought neither would do me much good), I had been turned into a college student, or at least a potential one.

After taking several night courses for credit I was allowed to matriculate as a regular undergraduate student in the Department of Science, Literature, and Arts. The sequence of fortunate events had whetted my appetite for more formal education. I was immeasurably helped by being given employment in a shop that rebuilt fuel pumps, windshield wipers, and shock absorbers for automobiles. My employer, Joseph Krawetz, himself a former immigrant from Russia, allowed me to work forty hours a week during times that fit into my program of classes at the university. That meant working after the regular shop hours and on weekends. Mr. Krawetz and his son Mayer, who ran the shop, trusted me with a key and my accounting of the hours that I put in at work.

My days started early with a carpool arrangement taking me to class on the Minneapolis campus of the University of Minnesota. By that time I was renting a room closer to work than the Weiller home and also within walking distance to and from the tram connections to the university. I was able to schedule all my classes in the morning and then catch a streetcar around noon for a forty-minute ride to work. Invariably, I fell asleep upon boarding the streetcar and awoke about three blocks before getting off for work. This neat arrangement was only good for going to work. It did not function on other occasions such as a late date when I failed to wake up at the appointed car stop and had to ride to the end of the line and wait for the next connection, sometimes an hour later.

It seems somewhat strange in retrospect that, in the face of my predominantly pleasant and satisfying experiences in the United States, I continued to be preoccupied with the belief system that I had brought with me to the new country. My ideological baggage, generated by living in Nazi Germany, by membership in the youth movement, and by exposure to the then dominant belief in Zionism as the only solution to the Jewish problem, continued to be core elements of my character. I was, in fact, surprised that wherever I found myself located in American society I encountered people who shared at least some of my beliefs and values. Not surprisingly there were others who took issue but rarely vigorously. More typically, acquaintances, work associates, and fellow students were indifferent toward my ideas, but that situation also left room for discovering areas of common interest.

Despite a tight schedule of full-time work and studies I went out of my way to find people who shared my labor-socialist Zionist views, and together, as a group of eight or ten, we managed to attract an organizer from New York who helped established a chapter of the *Hashomer Hatzair* movement in the Twin Cities (the reader will recall that there were branches in Palestine and several European countries, including Germany). Other like-minded people I found among customers of a progressive bookstore, liberal or left wing student associations, and graduate students in the social sciences. Having Mollie Weiller, nearly three times my age and a respected denizen of St. Paul, share many of my views gave me the feeling that my ways of thinking were not way out during the period preceding the country's involvement in World War II.

My most controversial orientation centered on the way I perceived the Soviet Union. I had indicated earlier that living in Nazi Germany, where Jews shared with the Soviets the attribute of being the most detestable creatures in the world, naturally predisposed one toward a favorable view of the " first socialist society." In Germany, all writings and pronouncements depicting the Soviet Union in terms other than the Nazi perspective were strictly banned. While still living there, our main source of information was an occasional visitor from abroad who had access to less biased sources of information.

I had grasped soon after my arrival in the United

States, however, that while freedom of speech, press, and other forms of expression were an intrinsic part of American culture, writings on the subjects of socialism, communism, and the Soviet Union did not present a balanced picture. Admittedly, the three are separate issues, but their presentation is often burdened with a heavy and widespread bias reflecting American mainstream ideology which heavily favors free-market capitalism, individual initiative, and reliance on self and family rather than the state. That belief system, however well-anchored it may be in American society, served as a basis prior to and following World War II for repressive forms of investigations of liberal and left-wing organizations by the House Committee on Un-American Activities and the Senate Hearings managed by Senator Joseph R. McCarthy (he was eventually censured by the Senate for abuse of senatorial privileges). The impression was created by spokespeople for these investigators that organizations and activities on the left pose a danger to the American system of government and way of life.

The differences between American mainstream beliefs and leftist ideologies alone, however, do not explain the congressional extremism and attendant excesses such as the banning of the Communist party, the anti-red inquisition in Hollywood, loyalty oaths in public universities, and campaigns of ideological cleansing in branches of government and the army. These extremist actions by American authorities reveal in no small measure the insecurity of a nation between two wars that had just emerged from the devastating Great Depression. Moreover, aversion to collectivism and socialist philosophy have deep roots in American history and are widely viewed as a threat to the American way of life.

In my own personal way, I never ceased being amazed by the fact that the average citizen seemed to take the authoritarian manifestations of red baiting in their stride. Henry Weiller, the husband of Mollie Weiller and a successful businessman but without interest in political issues, once took me aside with these words of caution: "I know how you feel about political things and I don't know who is wrong and who is right, but I do want to caution you that what you believe will endanger your becoming a citizen and keep your parents from joining you here." There was no malice in his words and I was convinced that he had my interest at heart. But I was also dismayed to realize that what he described represents essentially an undemocratic way of dealing with people, whether they are citizens or immigrants.

My personal ideology predisposed me toward a favorable view of the Soviet Union, not only because the Nazis viewed them as their chief enemy but also because in the wake of the Nazi invasion of Soviet land in June 1941, that nation appeared to be the only one with enough resolve and power to stop the Germans. The Nazi-Soviet pact that preceded their military collision upset me greatly, and I had found it difficult to accept the argument, advanced by the Soviets and their sympathizers abroad, that the pact was for them a stalling maneuver to buy time for the inevitable Nazi-Soviet confrontation.

The Soviet government's opposition to Zionism was a matter of record, and I was disturbed by it as well. Their answer to the international movement of Jewish renaissance, which they could not control, was a Jewish settlement in the Birobidzan region of eastern Siberia. The project never attracted many Jewish settlers and became devoid of meaning when Russian Jews acquired the option to make Israel their home.

Liberals and socialist sympathizers like myself accepted reports about Stalin's totalitarianism with a grain of salt by either casting doubt on the objectivity of the reporting source or arguing that autocracy was a necessary evil in the face of the external threats posed to the world's first socialist society.

My ideological journey met with a challenge from a person in authority, my first English instructor in the evening credit program of the University. He was a Ph.D. candidate in the English Department who taught introductory courses required of all students except those able to pass an exemption test. The instructor, Carl L., was a conscientious teacher who took pains to individualize students according to their specific learning needs (this was most helpful to me because after living in the country for less than eighteen months, I needed all the individualization I could get).

The major theme of the course was social and economic problems in American society, with Steinbeck's *Grapes of Wrath* serving as the centerpiece of readings. As a prospective sociology major, I found this focus of special interest, and I also appreciated Carl's point of view which I would have characterized as liberal and social-change oriented. I had several dinner invitations to his home and enjoyed the hospitality extended by him and his wife Margaret as well as the discussions that centered on political developments in Europe and America's step-by-step involvement in the European conflict.

Mollie Weiller, with whom I shared my university experiences, graciously invited the couple to dinner, and I remember the evening as a delightful and intellectually stimulating experience. Fortunately, I was in a position to return Carl's attention to my educational and social needs by giving him an occasional hand with his preparation for the German language examination (all Ph.D. student were then required to pass two language exams).

From time to time, I accompanied him after his English class, held in Saint Paul, to the streetcar that would take him to his home in Minneapolis. The conversation usually dealt with the war in Europe and the Nazi-Soviet pact about which, as stated earlier, I had great reservations. It seemed inconceivable to me that signing a treaty of friendship, however temporary, with Nazi Germany was an effective way to keep the German monster regime at bay. To me, a refugee from Nazi Germany, the only emotionally tolerable response was a united front aimed at the ultimate destruction of the Nazi war machine. Carl thought that my point of view failed to take into account the reality of the situation in which the Soviet Union was isolated and faced a threat not only from Germany but from the capitalist nations as well.

Lodged in my memory is a slogan Carl cited in relation to the idea of America joining the Allies in the battle against Hitler. The slogan, which presumably originated in World War I, states "The Yanks are not coming; let God save the king." Carl did not repeat the slogan after the German invasion of the Soviet Union.

Another subject we dwelled on frequently in our private conversations was the ever-expanding activities of the House Committee on Un-American Activities. Related to them were stories of people losing their jobs because of left-wing sympathies and arrests of veterans of the Lincoln Brigade who had participated in the Spanish civil war. There was one occasion when we were sitting on a bench waiting for the streetcar. Carl got up to look in the bushes behind us making certain that no one was hiding there listening to our conversation. My immediate reaction that this is flaky behavior stood in need of correction following Carl's later skirmish with the university administration.

My ideological naïveté was tested on the occasion of an invitation to dinner by Margaret who extended the favor also to a friend if I cared to bring one. I decided to include Jackie, a high school senior, who was involved with socialist groups, and whom I had dated on two or three previous occasions.

My plan for a stimulating evening misfired. It took Carl and Jackie only minutes to sniff out each other's political scent by mentioning the names of friends and political activists. Their widely divergent socialist orientations, tied as they were to the names of Stalin and Trotsky, left no room for dialogue or debate. The subject of discussion during the rest of the evening did not come within earshot of socialism and the war in Europe. Jackie never expressed any sentiment about the dinner party. Carl by contrast, commented that she was hopeless. I considered it then and to this day an immoderate statement but desisted from asking for an explanation.

At about the same time, most likely before the soiree at my professor's house, the class was given an assignment to analyze propaganda statements of two well-known political leaders. I picked the prime candidates for such an assignment, namely Adolf Hitler and Joseph Stalin. Carl liked my critical analysis of Hitler. Regarding my comments about Stalin he noted on my paper: "You don't believe all of this, do you?"

I received a C for the course, one of the few Cs during my college career, but the grade did not stand in the way of removing my probation status and allowing me to register as a regular day student. I am also firmly convinced that the grade was fair and that I did not deserve a better one. When I met Carl several months after completing his course and showed him papers submitted later in more advanced courses he applauded my progress.

There is a postscript to Carl's career as an English professor at the University of Minnesota. Before the end of the term in which I studied under him, he was informed by the administration that he would not be allowed to teach English in the future. The unofficial word that was leaked to him suggested that his communism stood in the way of future employment by the department.

Carl shared this information with the class and pointed out that communism clearly denotes membership in the party, a status that did not apply to him. He stated, furthermore, that insinuations based on hearsay cannot serve as a basis for administrative action. Following his announcement the class met without him and decided to take action as a group. I was one of two organizers of this move which generated a letter signed by all those present, comprising nearly everyone who had taken Carl's course. We expressed the view in writing that our professor was a dedicated teacher and that attending his classes was a positive learning experience. We also stated that removing him because of beliefs not shared by the broader public clearly constituted a violation of academic freedom. We declared furthermore that the dismissal of our professor would lead us to reconsider continued participation in the university's evening program (I am not sure how many of us were really willing to take that step).

About the time the term ended Carl was informed that

the English Department was retaining him as a faculty member, but he would be assigned to teach sub-freshmen courses. Members of the class were gratified by the news and declared victory. In the years following this event I lost touch with Carl except for the brief chance encounter mentioned above. Prior to my return from overseas service in the United States Army I wrote to his family and learned in a reply written by Margaret that Carl had resigned from the University and also the family and had signed up for a special service in the U.S. military forces (I don't remember the details).

Margaret invited me to visit the family, which now included two young daughters. I had known the older one as a toddler during the times I visited the family. It was she, now a four- or five-year-old, who seized hold of me when her mother was busy and declared in a loud voice: "My daddy left us and will never come back. Won't you stay here and be my daddy?"

3

Zionism, Reactive and Proactive

Attending the University of Minnesota on a full-time basis was for me a rewarding experience in every way. Although my schedule of morning classes and afternoon work did not leave much time to lounge around, I found myself in a stimulating atmosphere where asking questions was encouraged, and the expression of diverse and contrasting points of view was seen as enriching, not disturbing. Courses during the first year of full-time study comprised required subjects such as mathematics, English, a natural or physical science, social science as well as classes that would eventually lead to a major. Unscheduled time between classes would enable me to spend at the library or stop off at Hillel House, the Jewish student center, where more often than not I would meet an acquaintance, who like myself was in need of unscheduled sociability.

Classes in sociology afforded me an opportunity to develop a beginning perspective about the society in which we live and others that surround us. My interest in the subject dates back to a book which I had read, titled *The State* by Franz Oppenheimer (1926), who viewed conflict and exploitation as key processes in the development of the state. To a person like myself who was then living in Nazi Germany, this theory had immense appeal. I needed at this stage exposure to other formulations on the subject offered in the curriculum of the sociology department. It did not actually happen during the first year of full-time study because the courses available to me were basic, serving as prerequisites to those that constituted my major or area of specialization. The beginning courses in the social sciences, whether sociology, economics, or political science, made me realize that prevailing theories, whether widely accepted or lacking such support, represent attempts by the author to explain given phenomena and predict their future course. The question of the adequacy of such theories was a subject for graduate study which, in my case, had to be put off until my completion of military service, almost all of it outside the United States, that covered the period from December 1942 to October 1945.

During my stay in Minnesota I felt an intense concern about the rest of my family who lived close to the European theater of war. My sister Hedy, who had been selected for the children's transport to England, seemed to be doing well. After several months in congregate housing with other transport children, she was placed with an English family headed by the distinguished pianist, Angus Morrison. Hedy had the good fortune to find herself in a warm and accepting atmosphere. After a two- to three-year period she enrolled in a nursing course at the Princess Elizabeth Children's Hospital in London, which awarded her a degree in nursing. Other than that she was exposed, as was the rest of the English population, to the constant threat of bombardment from the German Luftwaffe and later in the war, from V-1 and V-2 rockets launched from the Continent.

My parents, trapped as they were in Germany by the

outbreak of World War II, had no longer any control over their lives. They attained sponsorship for future emigration to the United States by a generous businessman in New York City. But without any evidence of kinship, they were given a low priority on the waiting list. After America's entry into the war I found myself handicapped in attempts to help them because my official status had suddenly changed from recipient of first papers (and candidate for citizenship) to enemy alien. As an applicant for co-sponsorship on behalf of my parents, I was granted a hearing by a judge representing the Immigration and Naturalization Service in Washington, D.C. The interview went well, and he complimented me on my adjustment to life in Minnesota and expressed hope regarding their chances of coming to this country. But events in Europe overwhelmed any likelihood of rescue in the near future.

Following the outbreak of war between Germany and the European Allies, my parents were ousted from their apartment and forced into crowded living arrangements in the inner city of Mannheim. On the morning of October 20, 1940, they—together with over 6,000 other German Jews—were expelled from their homes in Baden-Wuerttenberg and crowded into seven trains for a forty-eight hour trip to Camp de Gurs in southern France alongside the Pyrenees mountains. (Zuccotti, 1993, p. 65). The deportees, many of them children and old people, arrived rainsoaked and shivering with cold, and were pushed into barracks without benches, mattresses, or straw. The hygienic conditions in the camps were abysmal, and the lack of food resulted in the death of many residents.

The internment camps were located in the segment of France under control of the Vichy government, which under its head, Marshal Philippe Petain, collaborated extensively with the German conquerors. While Vichy residence provided respite, however temporary, from direct contact with the Nazi authorities, the conditions of internment behind barbed wire with armed guards patrolling and muddy roads that turned into sewers during a rain, turned life into a living nightmare barely a step removed from the extermination camps.

In the summer of 1942, when mail from Vichy could still reach the United States, my father who was then held in Camp de Milles (my mother was still interned in Gurs) wrote to me that rumors pointed to an impending move and that he hoped that he would be together with my mother again. This was the last communication from my parents. Few outside the Nazi orbit knew that the next move would be a transport to the Auschwitz extermination camp. My parents were among the deportees of convoys nineteen and twenty-eight that left France in August and September of that year. I was not able to obtain documentary evidence until forty years later in a volume published by Serge Klarsfeld, *Memorial to the Jews of France* (1983), that described the deportation and mass murder of 80,000 Jews that had been living in France. The role of the Vichy government in the dreadful endeavor ranged from ready cooperation with the Nazis, supported by anti-Semitic legislation (targeting particularly the foreign-born French Jews) to reluctant complicity or delayed action in some instances (Klarsfeld, pp. XIII–XVI).

Nearly fifty years later the government of France agreed to pay compensation to the orphans of the victims of the French deportations. Among the parties specifically implicated in the crimes was the French railroad that had transported the West German Jews to the Vichy internment camps and ultimately to their doom.

During the year preceding my draft call I continued being active in youth Zionist organizations in the Twin Cities. For the first time, however, the question arose in my mind as to whether in the face of my emerging college education my youth movement ideal of living in a Palestinian Kibbutz was what I wished to do with my life.

My interest in the social sciences did not fit into the paradigm of the Labor Zionist movement which stressed a shifting of Jewish settlement in Palestine away from business and intellectual pursuits into farming and industrial production. Labor Zionism as articulated by Borochov (Avineri, 1981, pp. 139–150) considered it necessary for the Jewish population in the future Jewish state to be strongly represented in the working class, which he saw destined to establish a socialist society. This Marxist-based formulation is only one of several undergirding Labor Zionism, but one that wielded considerable influence on Jewish settlement in Palestine. The Borochov ideology held a strong grip on the international Zionist youth movement Hashomer Hatzair with which I had enjoyed extended associations in the past.

Borochov and Aharon David Gordon (Avineri, 1981, pp. 139–158) who spoke of the "religion of labor" (he shifted from a successful career as a manager of agricultural estates in Russia to a life of agricultural laborer in Palestine), both conveyed to would-be immigrants to Palestine the idea that the appropriate preparation for life in the Jewish homeland is training in farming or industrial production.

By the time I took day classes as a matriculated student at the University of Minnesota, it was becoming clear that the original Labor Zionist idea to which I had subscribed no longer represented a goal consistent with my experiences and development in the United States. In the first place my move in the past two years in an academic direction did not fit the paradigm of the rootless Diaspora Jew whose future was bound up with the peasantry and working class that would constitute the core element of the future Jewish state. I had begun to generate independent career ideas which Labor Zionists would have characterized as those of a *Luftmensch* or individual suspended in the air. Secondly, while the notion of becoming a farmer never had much appeal for me (at the time I was forced to seek a job because German public schools had ousted their Jewish students, I had opted for learning carpentry in preference to agriculture; such a job, however, did not materialize) I had developed serious doubts that any society even in its early stages of development could manage without having people employed in the fields of commerce and education.

I recall that several years later, after my return following army service, to the University of Minnesota, I presented the Labor Zionist premises regarding the need for the so-called normalization of the Jewish occupational structure to Professor Don Martindale, distinguished theorist and popular teacher in the Sociology Department. The salient proposition of the Labor Zionist thesis held that in most countries of the Diaspora the occupational distribution of the Jewish population represented an inverted pyramid in contrast to the structure of the non-Jewish citizenry whose makeup can be described as a normal pyramid. The latter is characterized by a stratification where farmers and industrial workers are at the bottom, white collar and service workers in the middle, and professionals at the top. The inverted pyramid model was viewed as not functional for the operation of an independent society and likely to thwart economic and political processes leading to a central political and social position of the working class.

Professor Martindale's off-the-cuff response pointed to the fact that Jews have had a long tradition of learning and scholarship, and that any Jewish society would be seriously remiss if it did not build on that tradition. He also raised some questions regarding the loose analysis on which the Labor Zionist argument was built. He, nevertheless, appeared to miss the point that the Labor Zionist ideology for nation building required core formulations that had emotional appeal in order to attract the necessary manpower and capital that provided the skills to dry swamps, produce food, construct housing and build highways, etc. These formulations were contained in A.D. Gordon's *Religion of Labor* precepts and Borochov's Zionist Marxism. Their credos, interacting with the widespread anti-Semitism in most countries of the Diaspora and the Nazi holocaust help explain the success of Jewish statehood resting on an adequate foundation of man-and-woman power.

Like other movements of national renaissance, Zionism had a basic underlying belief system that stressed the ingathering of the exiles (translated: bringing together all the Jews who are ready to live in the Jewish national homeland), the use of a common language (in this case Hebrew, the language of the Bible), the advancement of a common culture, and the creation of a political framework that would guarantee international recognition and protection against threats from without. Beyond this common denominator a number of influences would be seen to sustain the Zionist enterprise by bringing it under the common tent of national rebirth. Prominent among them are traditional Judaism, cultural, often referred to as secular, Judaism, nationalism stressing the concept of power, socialism, both utopian and revolutionary, and a variety of spiritual formulations associated with the names of leading philosophers such as Ahad Haam and Martin Buber.

My own format of Zionism, shaped mainly by the *Werkleute* youth movement, emphasized cultural Judaism and socialism which was a vague mixture of the Marxist version and Buber's utopian approach. My last months in Germany, as alluded to earlier, predisposed me increasingly toward the view that only a revolutionary endeavor could come to grips with a destructive force such as Nazi fascism. The similar features shared by the two certainly escaped me at that time.

During my third year in the United States most of my time was devoted to full-time work and full-time university study. I continued seeing Mollie and Henry Weiller at least once a week, generally responding to their gracious dinner invitations. There was time for dating, more often than not with girls I had met in classes or at Hillel House. Some of my contacts were with members of the Labor Zionist youth movement Habonim that held meetings in North Minneapolis. That group, in contrast to Hashomer Hatzair (with which I was associated just before leaving Germany and also in St. Paul where I helped set up a branch) disavowed revolutionary socialism but endorsed living in a Kibbutz. I was also affiliated with a campus Zionist organization, IZFA (the Intercollegiate Zionist Federation), which recommended Aliyah (or immigration to Palestine or Israel after statehood in 1948) but had no dominating political philosophy. The young people in these organizations were almost without exception American-born and well-adjusted to society. They joined Zionist groups because their friends were members or because of encouragement from the parents who themselves had then or in the past been associated with Zionism.

The American Zionism I encountered upon arriving in the United States naturally offers a striking contrast to the German Zionism during the Hitler regime. That is scarcely surprising, for after the Nazi takeover Zionism became a significant ideology and mechanism for survival. Although few German Jews were able to foresee or even imagine the occurrence of the Holocaust at the onset of the Hitler takeover, they had lost all hope in the future by the time of the proclamation of the Nuremberg Laws. Almost overnight Zionism became an ideology of hope even in the absence of an actual opportunity to settle in Palestine. Zionism affirmed simply—some historians may have said simplistically—that the only answer to worldwide anti-Semitism in its many forms is a Jewish state whose future is guaranteed by its citizenry.

Prior to the rise of Nazi-Fascism, Jews in western Europe in general and Germany in particular, viewed themselves as a product of the Enlightenment which conferred on them social equality or at least the right to equality. The preferred view of themselves held by many German Jews was that of "German citizens of the Mosaic faith." There was also a large segment of German Jews who played down or denied their Jewishness. The intermarriage rate in 1932 before the advent of Naziism had reached 60 percent. About 20 percent of the German Jewish population were eastern European nationals (Gribets, p. 398).

Zionism in Germany before 1932 was an ideology embraced mainly by elite groups such as rabbis, heads of religious and educational institutions, writers, publishers, and artists. Eastern Europeans were strongly represented among German Zionists by virtue of the fact that they came from backgrounds that offered Jewish full-time study and training for the rabbinate. Grounding in these subjects exposed them to Zionist ideology and also equipped them to become educators in Jewish educational and social institutions.

German Jews in the wake of World War I had come to see themselves as loyal citizens who had contributed to all aspects of Jewish life including the pursuit of war. Lingering as well as indisputable evidence of anti-Semitism tended to be met with denial and often the expression of hope that the Weimar Republic would sooner or later heal all wounds. The shock of events in 1933 was more than most assimilated Jews could handle and resulted, among other tragedies, in a disproportionate number of suicides. The Zionism embraced by many Jews during the Nazi years served as an antidote to the stereotype created by the Hitler propaganda machine of the rootless, scheming, cowardly Jew.

American Zionism, by contrast, was not the reactive or defensive type of ideology. Zionism was part and parcel of the great waves of Jewish migration from eastern Europe before and after the turn of the nineteenth century. It was rooted in religion as well as the broader tradition which championed the idea of Jewish continuity by means of a religious and cultural center in Palestine. In a nation composed of immigrants from all over the world, the notion of continued attachment to one's customs and way of life was not considered abnormal behavior or grounds for suspicion of disloyalty to the new country. American Zionism was proactive in its emphasis of building on the past and creating a homeland or state that would unite Jews in Palestine and the Diaspora. Although few of the Jews who had settled in the United States were giving serious thought to future resettlement in Palestine or Israel after the establishment of statehood in 1948, there appeared to be a general approval of persons committing themselves to *Aliyah*. Nonetheless, over the decades of the twentieth century, American *Aliyah* had amounted to a trickle compared to the waves of immigrants from other countries.

American Jews as a group, whether Zionist or not (it had been my impression that only a small minority were actively anti-Zionist), were not preoccupied with the issue raised by Sinclair Lewis (1935) in his novel *It Can't Happen Here* that deals with the rise and establishment of a fascist dictatorship in the United States. The predominant view among American Jews held that despite evidence of anti-Semitism, a subject closely monitored by the Anti-Defamation League, the United States Constitution and system of democracy provided guarantees against the violation of the human rights of its citizens.

This view obviously represents an optimistic perspective that paid little heed to America's treatment of its deprived minorities, native as well as foreign-born. The upbeat outlook, which is firmly embedded in American culture as a society of immigrants, was appealingly demonstrated in St. Paul, Minnesota prior to World War II in a Festival of Nations held periodically in the city's auditorium. The festival, which I attended not long after my arrival in the States, paid homage to ethnic groups represented in Minnesota by means of pageants, displays of ethnic artifacts, sale of native foods. and dramatic and dance presentations in indigenous customs. I was deeply impressed by the event by virtue of the atmosphere of good will and tolerance generated by the encounter and collaboration among diverse groups. This experience was worlds removed from the climate of ethnocentrism and racism that I had left behind.

The time period between Pearl Harbor and my draft call for army service was spent in work and full-time study. During the summer of 1942, a small group of friends who shared a Labor Zionist orientation but did not favor any formal organizational affiliation, met for picnics in the park and hikes along the banks of the picturesque St. Croix River. Planning for the future was on hold as the young men in the group anticipated new but still unknown roles related to the war which quickly enveloped all aspects of life in American society.

My draft number came up in the fall of 1942, but I applied for and easily received deferment until the end of the winter quarter—known elsewhere as a trimester—to complete my course work at the university. In the middle of December, I reported to Fort Snelling for physical and mental examinations. The latter revolved mainly around one question: "Do you like to go out with girls?" In response to my "yes" answer the lieutenant inquired further as follows: "When was your last date?" I answered truthfully but less than coherently, "tonight." He looked at me, but decided not to pursue the matter further.

At the end of the induction process, which also included close-order drill and making beds with hospital corners, we were given our orders for basic training in the art of war. My classification called for assignment as an interpreter, presumably based on my knowledge of German and reasonable ability to communicate in French. Together with two other soldiers classified as specialists, one a crane operator and the other trained in operating IBM machines used in the personnel classification process, I was given orders to report to Fort McClellan, Alabama for an eight-week course in basic infantry training. Why we had to travel from the far north to the deep south for a short basic-training course that was offered in camps all over the country was never revealed to us. But the few days in the army had already taught us "Yours is not to reason why."

A layover of several hours in Chicago enabled me to call Kurt and Marie Berg, good friends from my hometown Mannheim, who came to see me off without prior notice at the train departing for Alabama. Kurt and Marie had been co-leaders of one of the teenage groups of the Jewish youth community in Mannheim. The group held meetings at the homes of its members who included my brother, Siegbert. At one of the meetings hosted by my brother I was allowed to sit in and also share in the refreshments. I remember Kurt and Marie taking a special interest in me and letting me sit on their laps (the chairs were not high enough for me). In subsequent years, after my brother left for Spain, Kurt and Marie kept in touch with our family, and my ties with them were renewed and greatly strengthened when they settled in Chicago shortly before my arrival in Saint Paul. It was enormously reassuring to me to have them bid me farewell on my way into the unknown.

We three Minnesota "specialists," again on the train together and Alabama-bound, dreamed about the interesting assignments that awaited us after completing eight weeks of basic training. After all, there had to be a reason, we figured quite innocently, for the army to ship us on a forty-eight-hour journey on a civilian train, and that our special skills justified the investment in time and transportation.

What happened next provided us with a short course, not in basic training but fundamental socialization into army life. When we reported to the office of the commander of Fort McClellan we were informed that the eight-week course had been closed, and there were no vacancies for any of us. We were instead reclassified as soldiers in the heavy weapons infantry and placed in a thirteen-week course. We had no time to feel sorry for ourselves, for within an hour we were issued all the necessary training gear and assigned to our quarters.

There is nothing quite so unsettling as being told the "facts of life" by dissatisfied old-timers, defined as soldiers who arrived twenty-four hours earlier. We learned that Walter Winchell, well-known newscaster, had called Fort McClellan "the hellhole of the South," that the typical work day is between twelve and sixteen hours, and that there was not enough food in the mess hall to keep from being hungry all the time. End of a dream!

4

The Rhythm of Army Life: "Hurry Up and Wait"

If army basic training can be described as living in a total institution in the sense that Goffman assigns to a mental hospital (Clausen, 1959, p. 505), then Fort McClellan's basic preparation for the art of war represented a good example of that concept. Life was so highly controlled that no initiative was left in the hands of the trainees. The day started before dawn (this being January in Alabama) with a formation and flag raising, followed by breakfast, arranging the bunks, inspection of quarters, close order drill, classes in weapons training, five- and ten-mile hikes, and so forth, interrupted by a short period for lunch, and then more classes till supper.

Supper is best remembered in my mind for the shortage of food. At the end of the meal there was a frantic race to the PX (post exchange) to satisfy our hunger. On many evenings there were scheduled activities such as KP (kitchen police), cleaning heavy weapons. and various campground tasks. Unpleasant chores such as KP were often assigned as punishment for not passing inspection (i.e. an incorrect hospital corner on the bunk or not achieving the required score on the firing range). Similar "violations" might also cause weekend passes to be canceled.

The cause for the food shortage was not revealed, and questions posed to the non-commissioned officers in our unit were met with silence. Rumors had it that a black market operation was under way which diverted food destined for army personnel to civilian dealers. Judging by my three-year army experience, food shortages were a highly unusual situation in the United States Army, which always took pride in getting food to its personnel wherever they were located.

In my unit at McClellan we would jokingly refer to the lack of chow as the army's way of conditioning us to adversity as a means of surviving combat. In truth, it is hard to believe that the food shortage any more than other frustrating conditions encountered at the camp were ever part of a rational plan for military training.

Most of the non-commissioned officers in charge of the training program were southerners. They tended to form a special relationship with trainees from southern states granting special favors such as passes or exemptions from KP and other odious chores. The southerners, both noncoms and trainees, frequently expressed antipathy toward the other men in the unit who were, for the most part, New Yorkers. About half of this group were of Italian descent, the remainder were Jewish. Arguments between the members of the latter groups were common, often triggered by anti-Semitic remarks. (I myself was once involved in a fist fight following an anti-Jewish slur from a soldier of Italian descent.) A few of the Italian group expressed sympathy for Mussolini, while others pledged to desert if the U.S. army were to attack the Vatican.

Add this social situation to the demanding and strenuous schedule of training, and it becomes quite obvious that McClellan was closer to a nightmare than it was to building the skills and morale needed to fight a war. About a week after starting the program my body reacted intensely to the situation. I reported for sick call before breakfast because of a feeling that my legs could not support me. The medic took one quick look at me and called for transportation. I have no recall of what happened to me the next forty-eight hours. When I awoke the nurse told me that I had a severe case of the flu and needed to remain in the hospital for a while. My main concern was that my condition would keep me in basic training longer than the thirteen weeks required by the course. I did not have to worry much. When I returned to my unit, I found that in the anemic atmosphere that prevailed, nobody noticed my absence or cared how I would fit into the ongoing training program. As it turned out, every member of the unit graduated with the exception of one trainee, one of the oldest in the unit, who reportedly died as a result of suffering a heart attack while carrying the barrel of a 81-mm mortar.

The foregoing came to us as part of the rumor mill that flourished at McClellan in place of a system of sharing information that one would consider a precondition for maintaining morale among soldiers poised to enter combat. Indeed, within hours after completing the heavy weapons course we found ourselves on a troop train to Camp Shenango in Pennsylvania, which was at that time a major distribution center for army personnel. Members of our training company were widely scattered once they arrived at Shenango, but those I encountered during my brief stay were all in an upbeat mood following "liberation" from Fort McClellan.

Shenango made few demands, and we were issued

passes to visit family and friends prior to our next assignment. Saint Paul and Chicago were too far away for the time allotted, I opted for a visit to a *Hachsharah* (preparation for life in a Palestinian Kibbutz) farm in New Jersey, where I knew a few of the trainees. I found what I was sure I could count on: a warm reception, a sharing of common concerns, and the absence of a pre-dawn bugle calling for a day of rigid regimentation.

Upon returning to Shenango it was understood, though not officially articulated, conceivably for security reasons, that we would be quickly on our way to an overseas assignment. In southern Europe, particularly Italy, the initiative was in the hands of the Allies, and it was not far-fetched to think that the supply of armed personnel had the highest priority there.

What happened next defied anticipation by even the most imaginative mind. I found myself among a sizable contingent of troops heading east on a one-way railroad trip whose destination was not known to anyone of us. On the evening of that day we unloaded at a camp whose name I don't recall (we were there hardly long enough to merit remembering it) in the vicinity of Newport News, Virginia. Upon descending on the platform we found ourselves surrounded by a large number of armed MPs (military police) who accompanied us on the ride in trucks to the camp billets. Once inside the barracks every entrance and exit was guarded by the MPs who were under orders to keep us inside our quarters except for short bathroom trips, which they supervised as well.

The subsequent night left little time for sleep. Instead, we were subjected to batteries of medical tests and inoculations in preparation for the impending overseas assignment. Early the following morning, following a hasty breakfast, we were trucked to the harbor of Newport News for embarkation on a flotilla of LSTs (Landing Ship: Tanks). Only at the end of the gangway to the ship was our MP escort terminated.

A few hours later on the high seas a rumor was circulated that there had been a communication glitch and the Military Police believed we were a group of prisoners being transferred for assignment overseas. Since when, it must be asked, does the U.S. Army undermine its whole operation by sending unreliable personnel into the combat zone? How could the camp administration act without inspecting our service records, which were delivered with the troop transport?

It is in the nature of rumors that they defy efforts at investigation. They are statements being circulated whose origin is not known and whose connection to facts cannot be established. Some rumors arise spontaneously, representing perhaps wishful thinking or the expression of hostility to the prevailing beliefs. Other rumors, especially those planted by groups in power such as civilian and military bureaucracies, are designed to cover up either mistakes or nasty deeds that can not be defended. The latter may well apply to our own situation. The army, determined to maximize the shipment of personnel in the waning days of the North African campaign and the start of the battle for Italy, may have decided to employ raw police power to avoid AWOLs (absences without leave). If that was indeed the case, their attempt to cover up by the rumor that reached our ears was a uniquely inept. Not only was the story that circulated devoid of credibility, it also made the military authorities, who failed to inspect service records and had a problem communicating among is service branches, look incompetent. Not to mention the fact that the behavior of the Military Police and the explanations to cover up the so-called mistake were hardly designed to bolster the morale of soldiers on the way into combat.

The LSTs were landing craft designed for delivering heavy equipment and personnel on beaches in enemy territory. They were flat bottom vessels whose bow could be opened to disgorge its content in shallow water. The ship to which I was assigned carried a navy crew of about sixty and close to one hundred army personnel. The sleeping accommodations were for the most part bunkbeds placed in the ships' gangways. Our ship carried several tons of TNT packed in canisters that were strapped together.

All the LSTs traveled in a slow-moving convoy—reportedly at a speed of five or six knots an hour—accompanied by two destroyer escorts. This was not very reassuring in the face of reports of U-boat dangers circulating among the sailors manning the ships. As the convoy approached the Bermuda Triangle, our concern shifted from enemy action to forces released by nature. We encountered a heavy storm that tossed our flat bottom boats in towering waves. For reasons hard to fathom the senior army officer on our ship declared a pay day and asked us to line up for our wages. As my turn came I found the paymaster, a lieutenant, sitting helplessly in the middle of the cabin floor, surrounded by dozens of coins that were sliding from wall to wall. At precisely that moment, he declared "pay day postponed," and I found myself deprived of the financial resources which I had no place to spend.

Of further concern to us was the fact that the rocking and rolling motions of our ship led to the untying of the canisters which then slid from side to side of the cargo hold in rhythm to the pitching of the LST. As we lay awake at night, listening to the crashing sounds of the canisters, our imagination ran wild with thoughts about the explosive potential of the load we were carrying.

The entire LST convoy pulled into Bermuda harbor and remained there for about a week to rearrange cargoes, repair damage to boats, and generally prepare for the long haul across the Atlantic. Soldiers and many sailors were given liberty to visit Hamilton and beaches on the island. The Bermuda interval provided us with an unexpected but most welcome interlude of rest and recreation.

Our main contacts on shore were with American Navy personnel, who volunteered the information that among a number of LST convoys which had crossed the Atlantic in recent months, not a single one had arrived in North Africa without losses caused by German U-boats. Whether this was true or not could clearly not be verified—the actual information available to the American command would necessarily be treated as top secret. What puzzled us, however, was why a handful of securely shore-installed sailors would be so eager to send us on our way with a gloomy view of our future. Did their routine assignments on the island call for some emotional kicks from worried soldiers in transit?

The following three weeks of voyage to a yet undisclosed destination—it turned out to be Oran, Algeria—passed very slowly in view of the fact that we had little to do, yet were constantly aware of the danger lurking in the ocean below. To introduce some structure into our daily schedule somebody in the command system came up with the bright idea of having us line up on deck during dawn and dusk alert (when the U-boats were most likely to strike) with rifles at the ready. The plan called for firing at any approaching torpedo with the goal of exploding it before it could strike home.

I don't know whether this defensive maneuver could have been effective because it never had to be tested on our voyage. There were several instances of depth charges being dropped by one of the destroyer escorts, but no word reached us whether U-boats were actually sighted or only suspected of being close by.

One of the boats in our convoy ran into a potentially serious problem. (This was reported to me by one of the few friends I had made at Fort McClellan, who traveled on that particular vessel.) Its commander was a naval officer by the name of Goodrich who had authored a book telling the story of a destroyer in World War I. In the middle of the Atlantic the engine of this LST broke down, and it was decided to abandon the convoy for extensive repairs. There it sat, alone, unprotected in the middle of the ocean. At this point the captain called passengers and crew on deck for a public prayer. My friend, an agnostic, experienced no boost in his morale while his boat was a drifting, sitting duck in submarine-infested waters. Whether God or good luck was on their side will remain an open question, but the positive role of the ship's engineers is not in doubt. The boat caught up with the convoy within twenty-four hours.

On the voyage from Bermuda to North Africa we were spared further storms, and mild weather allowed us to spend extended time on deck. I chose for myself to spend several nights topside, rolled up in a blanket in a quiet corner. During the days I volunteered to do some cleanup work in the officers' mess. This provided me with access to a phonograph and a collection of classical music records. I was not allowed to do any waiting on tables, for this activity was reserved for a black member of the crew. Job segregation was still the rule in the Navy in 1943, and it confined African-Americans to low-level jobs. The Army was just beginning to place blacks in higher level positions including officerships, but their service was generally confined to separate units.

On the voyage to North Africa I became friendly with a navy crew member, who shared with me an interest in liberal politics. We both happened to be reading Wendell Willkie's *One World* (1943), published after his defeat by Franklin Delano Roosevelt in the 1940 presidential elections. This book was a strong plea for postwar international cooperation. We would sit or walk on deck talking for hours about our notions of how the United States and the Soviet Union might get along in a post-war world. My friend, being of Russian descent, was particularly concerned that the Soviet Union should emerge as a society toward which children and grandchildren of immigrants could express a sense of pride.

With great relief we arrived in Oran, Algeria. Thus ended our worry about being easy targets for German U-boats. Moreover, after four weeks of rocking and rolling travel on a flat bottom boat, the feeling of solid ground under our feet had a magic of its own. We had barely tied up in Oran harbor when the sirens sounded indicating that German planes had taken to the skies. Those of us already on land or close to the gangplank dashed to the nearest building for shelter. Other than the sound of our anti-aircraft batteries, I had no idea of the nature of the engagement between the enemy planes and our own forces. But this first wailing of the sirens impressed me mainly as a symbolic welcome to the arena of the land war.

Next we were unloaded in a transit camp in the vicinity of the city of Oran. A contingent of soldiers, who like myself had received infantry training, were addressed by a colonel, presumably the camp commander, on the purpose of being there. "Welcome to the camp of casuals whose mission is to replace those who made good in the war." I don't remember much of the rest of the speech, but it did end with an admonition to "keep your head low."

The thought occurred to me that they must have a special mission in mind for me since I was technically still an enemy alien. Before leaving Newport News I contacted a Jewish chaplain and explained to him my problem of going into combat without being an American citizen. He replied that I should not worry and that everything would be taken care of, or words to that effect. I learned within the next few days that the U.S. Army had no problem bestowing citizenship posthumously if there is no time for that ceremony before meeting the great reaper. Speaking for myself I had a clear preference on this matter.

As it turned out Uncle Sam probably did too. Within a period of approximately two weeks I was called away from duty in the kitchen—one of the few assignments given to casuals—and guided to the tent of a warrant officer, a Mr. Hazard, who, I learned, was a representative of the U.S. Immigration and Naturalization Service. He informed me unceremoniously that he was about to make me an American citizen. I looked at my soiled, government-issued clothing and my greasy hands with an obvious look of embarrassment. Mr. Hazard, aware of my state of mind, smiled and said, "Pay no attention."

The ceremony started with a question. "Do you know any person in this camp who has known you most of your life." When I looked at him in puzzlement as if to say you must be kidding, he said "Never mind, I shall take care of that." He stepped outside the tent and grabbed two GIs who happened to be walking by and declared in an authoritative voice "You have known this man (myself) all your life, right?" and not waiting for an answer declared, pointing to a prepared form, "Sign here and you are free to go." The rest of the process lasted but a few minutes, and I was also free to go in my greasy and tattered uniform but with a brand new status and a very good feeling.

Only a few days passed before I received my assignment to join an airborne, anti-aircraft unit at an undisclosed location (which turned out to be southern Sicily). The opportunity to exchange my position as a casual for permanent membership in a military unit appealed to me. However, as much as I searched my mind, I could not recall having received any training, not even one lecture, on airborne warfare. But that concern was overshadowed by the prospect of acquiring a domicile, whether lofty or earth-bound—I could call my home.

A few days later, I found myself on a train to Tunis, then on a ship to Palermo, Sicily, and finally on a truck to the southern coast of the island. The unit to which I was assigned was bivouacked in a cottonfield near Gela, where the company had come ashore in the American amphibious invasion of the island, The company commander extended a friendly welcome to our small group of replacements that arrived together. When he noticed that my military point of origin was Fort Snelling, Minnesota, he said "A Swede, eh?" to which I replied "No, a Jew," and he quickly retorted "A Jewish Swede, then." I thought this was an auspicious beginning, and I found my impression supported by my experience in that unit.

The members of my squad appeared to be a relaxed lot who seemed to enjoy each other's company. The atmosphere drew strength from the squad leader, who was supportive of his men and had a delightful sense of humor. A sense of humor was greatly needed several nights after my arrival when we occupied a new bivouac site in a flat area below a plateau on high ground on which there was an array of farms and small houses. The location of the buildings should have signaled to us a need to examine our choice of a camp site on low ground, but for some unknown reason we failed to do so.

In the early hours of the morning we were awakened by a sudden downpour, and moments later I found myself floating on top of the water in my bomb-bay door I had been using as a bunk after removing it from a downed German bomber. Within minutes the company found themselves in the middle of a lake whose depth varied from two to three feet. Bedding, tents, knapsacks, rifles, jeeps and other equipment were either underwater or floating all over the area. One member of our squad discovered that he was sharing his bomb-bay door bunk with a large snake of unknown origin. He ended the cozy (for the snake) arrangement with a burst of Tommygun fire, which most of us considered clearly a case of overkill.

In fairness to whomever selected the bivouac site it may be said in his defense that he was not in a good position to predict the rains, which arrived early in that fall of 1943. We all felt good that there was no finger pointing despite the fact that much of our equipment had to be replaced.

Until the arrival of new orders for future military engagement, we took advantage of frequent passes to visit nearby towns, go swimming, or relax at a time when the war seemed to be far away. The officers in the company emerged with the bright idea of scheduling a mini-Olympiad as a way of killing time, keeping us out of trouble, or perhaps promoting fitness. Participation was mandatory even for the couch potatoes. I don't recall much enthusiasm for the games, which, of necessity, had to be carried out without special equipment using whatever improvisation. The accepted, sports uniform could be underwear and army boots. My memory is vague on details except for the fact that the Sicilian Olympics were my finest hour. As a former sprinter, I helped my platoon to two victories: one in the hundred-yard dash and the other in the hundred-yard relay.

In short order, our unit found itself in a truck convoy to the north coast of Sicily. We pitched our tents in a staging area preparatory to an airborne mission. We were given no details, but our gear was packed into gliders, and we were kept in a state of readiness for the assignment. Particulars about the mission emerged only after its cancellation. The plan had called for a landing in gliders behind the enemy lines in the Rome area.

The Italian surrender to the Allies in August 1943, negotiated between General Eisenhower and Marshal Badoglio, guaranteed the availability of airfields around Rome for the landing of Allied divisions including our airborne unit. Before the Allied move could be carried out the Germans moved contingents of its army to the Rome area, and the Allied landing had to be called off.

When we realized that we had just been spared involvement in a dangerous mission we spontaneously reacted in a variety of ways to celebrate life. Some went on passes to Palermo, others relaxed with a bottle or two of wine, while a buddy of mine and myself decided to conquer a steep mountain overlooking the Thyrrenian Sea. I am not quite sure why we chose this mode of celebration, Neither one of us had much climbing experience, and we had no special equipment for the undertaking. A wish to celebrate by showing off may be the best explanation.

Members of our platoon acknowledged our climbing plans with incredulous looks suggesting that we had gone off our rockers. We pledged to chart the progress of our adventure with smoke signals every hour

The first two hours proceeded without difficulty, and we ignited weeds and dead wood to convince our buddies in the bivouac area that we were sticking to our plans. At the end of the third hour we dispensed with the signals, for we were much too busy selecting the right crevasses on the steep stone wall for a continued upward trek. By the middle of the fourth hour our climb had slowed to a crawl, and we debated whether an immediate descent would pose greater risks than an assault on the summit. The position in which we found ourselves made both options about equally unattractive, and we had to admit to ourselves that we were simply "stuck" near the top of the mountain.

It was precisely at this point that we heard a voice from above, which might as well have been from heaven, calling, "*salve*," the Italian equivalent of hi or hello. We then saw a face peering from behind a boulder, and a body extended its arms and made hand gestures, pointing the way out of our lofty prison. Our savior was a goatherd who brought his flock for grazing at the top of the mountain and seemingly knew it like the palm of his hand.

The rest was easy. We reached the summit, found a rock on which a number of GIs had engraved their names, and naturally added our own. We discovered that there was another trail to the mountain peak, perhaps ten times the distance we had covered in our ascent but free of any demanding climbs. We utilized the long and safe road home, returning to our camp several hours after dark. Nobody took note of our adventure, and we volunteered no information. We had learned that in a war you can live dangerously even if you are dozens of miles from the front.

In the wake of the Allied invasion of the Italian mainland we anticipated orders to join the march up the peninsula. That by itself would spell good news, because any northbound movement would indicate that the fight was being brought closer to the Nazi homeland and simultaneously to the end of the war.

Sicily had offered few opportunities for us to get to know the local population. The poverty on the island appeared overwhelming. The lack of food was pervasive, forcing some fathers to "rent out" their daughters as prostitutes for GIs in return for canned goods. I am left with the unforgettable recollection of long lines of prisoners who had surrendered to the U.S. Army and would be shipped out taunting us with comments such as "We feel sorry for you to be fighting a war over here, while we will be safe in America."

After the fall of Naples, our company was ordered to furnish anti-aircraft protection on a hill below a mansion overlooking the harbor. Despite the occasional sound of warning sirens there was little hostile activity in the area other than German reconnaissance planes beyond the reach of our artillery. My job called for attending to communications functions at the switch board or connecting and maintaining telephone lines between our battery and selected points in the Army network. The latter required me to string telephone wires across a populated area of the city. The work, while neither interesting nor challenging, led to many contacts both intended and accidental, while doing street-level work and climbing from roofs to balconies. While some residents expressed surprise at our appearance out of nowhere, they were generally cooperative and showed pleasure at our having replaced the Nazi army.

Naples was a scenic and culturally appealing city. There was the San Carlo Opera, orchestral concerts, museums, historic buildings, and voices from windows singing tunes of Italian grand operas. In the absence of enough work for the gun crews the commander of our battery devised a plan to improve the esthetic work environment. We were to paint selected rocks in the vicinity of our gun positions white. None of the enlisted men dared raise questions about the wisdom of an act that runs counter to all laws of military camouflage. The crew came up with two possible explanations. The officer was asleep when the subject was dealt with in the officers' training program. Or, alternatively, this was a clever scheme to fool the enemy aviators into believing that the hill was undefended, which was no more than a trap to draw them into the battery fire. The idyll of life on a landscaped slope in Naples soon ended. In late November 1943 our unit joined others in training for an amphibious invasion.

In the face of the sharp resistance offered by the regrouped German army along the Gustav Line—anchored by heavily fortified Cassino—the Allied march up the Peninsula had come to a stop. It was clearly a matter of time before a new strategy would have to be evolved to break the Nazi stranglehold on the "soft bottom" of southern Europe. The members of our unit would have been greatly surprised if they had not been called on to play a part in that strategy.

5

Reflections on What Used to Be Home

The lull in activities prior to our next engagement in the Italian campaign, the invasion of Anzio, gave me time to reflect on the fate of my family since the destruction of the Weimar Republic and the ascendancy of the Hitler regime. About a decade had passed since then, and the process of dismantling the family had been underway for some six years, starting with the departure of my brother Siegbert for what was thought to be a safer environment in Spain.

In November 2001, when returning with my wife Shirley from a two-week Elderhostel tour of Tuscany, we happened to fly over Lake Lugano, a well-known Swiss resort, where my parents had spent their honeymoon. It struck me then, as it had done repeatedly in the past, that their blissful start of matrimony was short-lived. They were not destined to lead a peaceful, gratifying family life. Events over which they had no control stood squarely in the way.

Not that my parents did not do all the right things before settling down. My father, ten years older than my mother, worked about a decade and a half until he had earned enough money to buy furniture for an apartment and merchandise to supply a retail establishment, which turned out to be a shoe store. My mother, prior to getting married, spent time in Paris to study dressmaking, a skill which not only met some of the family's clothing needs but, after the demise of the store, provided the major share of the family income.

According to plan, my parents settled in Mannheim, opened a shoe store in the inner-city and rented a three-bedroom apartment within a block of their establishment. The large apartment was designed to accommodate at least three children.

The first obstruction in the way of their carefully nurtured plans for the future was the outbreak of World War I. My mother was pregnant when my father was drafted for service in the Corps of Engineers. His departure forced my mother to take over the running of the store. Except for some brief furloughs my father was away from home for the duration of the war which raged from late summer 1914 till November 1918. I recall my mother telling me that at one of the visits Siegbert reacted to his father's arrival with the words, "Who is this man here?"

The loss of the war resulted in a general impoverishment of the German population. The government attempted to cope with the economic situation by printing paper money, giving rise to what came to be known as the German hyperinflation that reached its peak some five years after the war's end. At that point a hundred billion paper marks had the same purchasing power as the pre-war mark, which was worth twenty-nine cents. I remember my parents telling me that money earned had to be spent immediately to avoid loss of much of its value in the course of one night, and that workers had to be paid daily to keep spending in line with the inflation rate.

I entered the family picture in 1921, my sister Hedy arrived three years later. The family in which we grew up struggled to make ends meet. We managed to live within our means by budgeting carefully and avoiding unnecessary expenditures. Family life was anchored in the Jewish religion taking the form of membership in a synagogue whose religious orientation was liberal ("liberal" corresponding roughly to a position slightly more conservative than American "Reform"), observance of holidays, children's attendance of Hebrew school, and celebrating the Sabbath, which included a special Friday night meal, sometimes followed by going to Friday night services. To mark the Sabbath my mother baked every Friday two loaves of milk bread, a delicacy particularly for us children. To be precise, my mother prepared the dough, but the baking had to be done at a neighborhood bakery because our kitchen lacked an oven with enough space to accommodate the loaves (the only oven in our kitchen was coal-fired).

Family life followed a similar routine and regularity. There were few vacations or trips for the parents, not only because they were tied to the store but because they could not afford it. I recall only one occasion when my mother went to a spa in the Black Forest with me while my father joined us over the weekend. We children, however, were sent to summer camp a number of times and also to stay with out-of-town relatives before we were old enough to make our own arrangements within the framework of the youth movement.

Our birthdays were occasions for parties and gift giving. Presents of greater value were bestowed on us when our uncle Wilhelm (Guillermo), my mother's brother and his wife Selma, came on a visit from Spain where they had made their home. At such times the whole family was treated to meals at restaurants and trips to diverse places in taxis. I recall that prior to such visits I did extensive window shopping just in case my uncle asked for my preference regarding a present.

The education of the children was given priority. It was decided that the boys would attend middle school (Hedy was too young at the time when Jewish children were still eligible to study in middle school). This was the alternative to the mandatory eight-year primary school education; a high tuition was required during the period between the two world wars; this was a financial burden for my parents especially when added to the monetary assistance they provided to three surviving grandparents.

The shoe store was a marginal enterprise during the years of inflation and the subsequent economic recession. To supplement family income my father spent many hours on the road as a traveling salesman, marketing commercial calendars and stainless steelware. Frugality is probably what best describes the running of the family home. As already indicated education and the well-being of family members including the extended family were given precedence, and parents as well as children once they left school were expected to contribute to the family budget. We lived in a spacious, well-furnished apartment albeit in a somewhat rundown neighborhood in the inner city of Mannheim. As mentioned before, its location was chosen primarily for its proximity to the store. We inhabited what would now be considered a cold-water flat—it lacked central heating, and hot water for baths was generated by means of a gas heater. Coal for the oven in the kitchen and the stoves in each room had to be brought up five flights of stairs from the basement. On a typical winter day, only the kitchen was kept warm while blankets and featherbeds were the main protection against the low temperature in the bedrooms. The apartment contained a large icebox but no refrigerator. There was no family car. There were bicycles for the children and streetcars and trains for everyone to cover distances beyond walking range.

The present reader may conclude that the lifestyle described here is evidence of a low standard of living even by the criteria applied in the 1930s. That would be true when measured by American standards, but judged by conditions then prevailing in Germany that judgment would be an overstatement. Moving in 1939 from an urban setting to a similar one in the United States, I was struck by the much greater affordability in the United States of private housing, consumer credit, electric household appliances, and automobiles. There were, of course, some indices pointing in the other direction such as German national health insurance, but in the aggregate the advantage pointed in America's direction.

Neither my brother nor I ever challenged the notion that children should help out financially when the family is in need. My brother at one point bargained successfully for keeping a larger share of his monthly salary. I was satisfied with the 10 percent I retained, owing to the fact that I was younger and had less need for pocket money. It must be remembered that in the culture in which we grew up, reciprocal responsibility among the generations was widely accepted. That certainly extended, as shown earlier, to the grandparents even though my own family's income was not adequate to meet the needs of both children and grandparents.

While at home all of us shared an interest in music, although we pursued it in different ways. The adults were members of the *Liederkranz*, a Jewish choral group that had a professional director and participated in the performances of religious and secular works including the Hannukah cantata, "Light and the People" composed by the local cantor Hugo Adler with lyrics by the renowned Mannheim rabbi Max Gruenewald. This composition received both national and international exposure and earned long, standing ovations. My brother and I had the chance to sing in the children's choirs of various compositions. Siegbert and Hedy also were given piano lessons. An upright piano graced our living room and was one of the early purchases in our parents' marital life.

All of us children were at one time or another members of the Jewish youth movement, whose activities assigned great importance to making music by way of group singing as well as periodic musicales that featured those members who had acquired a beginning level of musicianship by taking lessons in piano, violin, and recorder.

The bond between us—children on the one hand and parents on the other—was weakest in the realm of ideology. This situation was alluded to earlier, reflecting above all divergent cultural influences affecting the two generations. My parents had lived through a devastating war and were firmly convinced that my father had done his duty but did so for a just cause. We children, even before the advent of Naziism, shared the view of many young people, particularly those associated with the German youth movement (excluding, however, members of nationalist organization), that the first great war was a conflict without ethical rhyme or reason, the result of economic and political rivalries among the great powers. We scoffed at the expression of patriotism in literature and music and treasured the songs of the youth movement that idealized peace, equality, and the creation of a better world.

The ideological differences within the family never led to arguments or extended efforts at persuading the other party. The Zionism of the children represented the views of the Jewish youth organizations which recruited young Jews with an ideology that held out hope for the future. The great attraction of Zionism was its affirmation of life in a new land, Palestine, in contrast to a blind trust in the status quo or refuge in an unknown country.

At the time when the Weimar Republic first fell victim to the deadly assault by the Nazi dictatorship, our parents still held fast to the belief that German Jews were German citizens of the Jewish faith. During the progression of events that included anti-Jewish boycotts, the proclamation of the Nuremberg laws, and the pogroms known as *Kristallnacht*, our parents' faith in the possibility of survival under the Nazi regime was severely shaken, and they initiated efforts to get their children out of the country. Until their deportation to France in 1940, they still nursed some hope that things might change for the better, especially for those who fought for the "fatherland." With the start of the war the tragic reality set in that there were few opportunities to escape.

The idea of a Holocaust or mass murder of the whole Jewish community could be visualized by few of the Jews who had lived among the Germans for generations. I have a photograph of my father, taken after he was released from Dachau following several weeks of brutal treatment. He is sitting at the kitchen table, dressed in a suit and tie, with a bottle of wine and a serene smile as if to say, well, the worst is over.

As I attempt to enumerate landmark events in the life of my parents I am struck by how the few happy occasions such as their marriage and honeymoon, the birth of three children, and about a decade of near normal family life were overshadowed by tragic circumstances. These included World War I, a mega-inflation, an economic depression, the Nazi boycott of Jewish businesses, the death of a son in Dachau, the departure for England and the United States of their remaining children, followed in quick succession by a forced move to a Jewish ghetto in their hometown, deportation to internment camps in southern France, and a second deportation to the death camp of Auschwitz.

I returned to Mannheim as a member of the Signal Intelligence Service shortly after the city was captured by the American Seventh Army in late March, 1945. Because of the destruction of the single Rhine bridge in the Mannheim area, we crossed the river at a point south of the city near Worms. Mannheim, a major industrial center and inland harbor, lay virtually in ruins. The captain of our unit furnished me with a jeep to make a detour and visit to the neighborhood where my former home was located. Throughout my family's stay in the city—which covered the period from their marriage in 1913 until their forced evacuation to a Jewish ghetto in 1940—they had lived in the same apartment in the inner city. The apartment house, one of the newer buildings erected early in the century, still stood with only minor damage, in contrast to most of the structures on the same block, which had either been destroyed or severely damaged by the sustained bombing carried out by the Allied forces.

In the company of a fellow soldier of my unit I climbed

the three flights of stairs and gained entry into our fourth floor apartment. A young person in work clothes did not resist our intrusion since we were in uniform and armed with carbines. I attempted to explain the purpose of our visit in three languages, but there was no response in a tongue we could understand. The man's looks revealed fear about our intentions which was hardly surprising. We were told later that several of the residents of the apartment house were displaced persons resettled from a D.P. camp. When we walked through our former apartment I saw that my parents' furniture had been removed. More details emerged over time such as the forced evacuation without prior notice of all local Jews to a temporary ghetto at the start of the war and deportation following the fall of France under the most brutal conditions.

We descended two floors and rang the bell at the apartment of the landlord. The reader will remember that the man had sheltered a Jewish resident during the *Kristallnacht* pogrom at considerable risk to himself. He was away at work, but his housekeeper, Agnes, after a searching and incredulous look at my face fell around my neck with tears pouring from her eyes. She said she had been terribly concerned about all of us ever since my parents were taken away and had feared the worst might have happened. Unfortunately, I had no news for her other than the events involving my sister and myself.

While our unit remained in the vicinity of Mannheim I visited the headquarters of our military government with two objectives in mind: to search for Hermann Hauser, the distant relative who had provided me with a job before my departure to the United States, and to hand in a small list of local individuals worthy of special consideration from denazification courts because of their mistreatment of Jewish students. I was in no position to follow up on the latter, and in retrospect, can view it now as no more than a symbolic act to remind myself that the past must not be buried.

I lucked out clearly, however, with the first task I had set for myself. The U.S. Army's governor of Mannheim knew Hermann, who had served as the last president of the Jewish community from early 1940 until the shutting down by the Nazi regime of all Jewish activities in the wake of the mass deportations which took place on October 22 of that year. Hermann was married to a non-Jewish woman. This fact gave the couple the status of a mixed marriage which in Nazi jargon was defined as a legal bond between a Jew and an Aryan. I am not sure whether the distinction between regular Jewish marriage and mixed marriage was spelled out in Nazi law or was an administrative arrangement made arbitrarily and on the spur of the moment. I do recall that categories of discrimination were in use with regard to education, housing, food rationing, etc. In the case of the deportation of Jews from the Rhineland, mixed marriages and their children, referred to a *Mischlinge* (half-castes), were exempted from the initial transports.

For Hermann and his wife Dora, my sudden emergence from a U.S. army vehicle was a somewhat unsettling experience. I had grown in height since they last saw me. They found it difficult to picture me in an American army uniform, and hard to grasp that there could be a sudden connection with a seemingly lost past. Hermann had worked as the administrator of the Jewish school and also taught some classes. When the school was closed down he was drafted for work in a labor battalion. Throughout this period of backbreaking work he had no assurance of being spared from eventual deportation (the Nazis were known to break up couples and send the Jewish partner to extermination camps). Hermann and Dora had been waiting for liberation from day to day, constantly in fear of being included in "the final solution." I was their first face-to-face contact with a person representing the other world from which they had been cut off nearly six years earlier.

Hermann was the last person I know to have been in contact with my parents at the start of the deportations from Mannheim. He provided whatever help he could render, especially for the elderly, at the loading platforms. Prior to their expulsion my parents had been sharing living quarters with the Hausers in the hastily set up local Jewish ghetto. When we met, their first questions had to do with the fate of my parents. Unfortunately, we could share no more than confessions of total ignorance.

6

Anzio—A Mediterranean Beachhead

When I joined my permanent army unit on the Italian island of Sicily as a replacement, most of its members had already been through an amphibious invasion, the one that opened the Sicilian campaign, The group, originally trained to function as an airborne battery, had barely missed being sent on a glider invasion in the Rome area after the fall of Mussolini. The plans for this mission were changed when, contrary to expectations, Nazi troops occupied the areas where the landing was to take place. There was a general understanding, based mostly on rumors, that the coming mission would again be of the amphibious variety. While stationed in Naples to protect the harbor area with anti-aircraft guns, we did indeed enter training for a landing at an unspecified location.

I had come to feel reasonably at home with the men in the battery, although there was no one in particular with whom I formed bonds or shared interests. My buddy, defined as the person with whom you share a pup tent, foxhole or dugout, was Mac (short for MacDonald), a southerner from a small town, with a cheerful disposition. We had fun upgrading successive dugouts on the beachhead to the point where we joked about renting our "real estate" to tourists after the war. Our only disagreement was on the subject of African-Americans about whom Mac had all kinds of reservations including their role in the military. He countered my opposing views by saying that since I lived in Minnesota I didn't really know "them."

One night in the third week of January 1944 we were brought to an assembly point in the Naples area and boarded an LCT (landing craft tank), a roll-on, roll-off shallow draft vessel for unloading vehicles and personnel on to beaches. After about an hour at sea the captain of our unit informed us that we were scheduled to land at h-hour plus one or about and hour after the first troops hit the shore near the town of Anzio. It emerged later that our invasion was designed as a bypass operation to relieve the pressure on the Allied armies composed of American, British, French and Polish divisions which had been halted on their march up the Italian peninsula. The most famous of the battles had been raging at Cassino where, despite the heaviest of air bombardments, the Allied forces had been beaten back. The Anzio invasion was designed to relieve the pressure on the troops driving north and arrayed on an axis between the Tyrrenian and Adriatic seas that came to be known as the Gustav Line.

Our landing was uneventful. When the ship's bow opened we stepped off a platform into knee-deep water and rushed ashore. It was at this point that I experienced my first real air raid. A group of German fighter planes, flying at a low altitude, dropped bombs and raked the beach with machine gunfire. Some two hours later, when making my way over a stretch of the beach, I witnessed the devastating evidence of the early morning raid: a group of bodies, some dismembered, laid out by the medics of the units that had suffered the casualties.

The next few hours were spent digging gun sights, stringing telephone wires, and preparing dugouts for protection against whatever was going to be thrown at us. At that point we had only the vaguest notion about what was happening on the total beachhead and in the areas surrounding it. We knew that at the moment landings of men and supplies proceeded at a rapid rate and that on the beaches just east of us near the town of Nettuno the British were disembarking and seizing ground in coordination with our effort. The combined bridgehead, we learned later, was about eighteen miles long and its depth half that size. Upon landing we noted with dismay the existence of a mountain range, known as the Alban Hills, that paralleled the seashore, but how these figured in the strategy of the invasion was initially unclear to us.

Not too many days passed before we realized that whatever may have been the strategy of the high command, the actual events were taking a different turn. On the days immediately following the landing the weather deteriorated. The unloading of supplies was halted or reduced to a bare minimum. Shells aimed at us began to land all over the beachhead, and they did so at an ever accelerating pace. We realized quickly that there was not a speck of land, or water for that matter, on the Allied terrain that could not be reached by the Nazi guns. These were the infamous eighty-eight millimeter, we were told. The artillery bombardment emanated, of course, from the Alban Hills which were firmly held by the Nazi army and provided countless observation posts for the enemy to note the results of their shelling.

One night following our landing we witnessed a most

terrifying scene—the explosion of a warship, a British destroyer, about half a mile off the beach where we were dug in. Equally overwhelming was the sight, several weeks later while working near the frontline, of one of our medium bombers hit by German anti-aircraft fire. The plane fell to the ground behind enemy lines. The wings and front fuselage came crashing down whereas the tail, which had broken off, descended with successive 360 degree rotations. Our inevitable reaction to such events was fear and compassion for the people involved and a feeling of helplessness over one's inability to lend a hand.

At some point which I cannot pinpoint in time we were alerted to the possibility that we might have to evacuate the beachhead. Since we had not been able to make a quick and early thrust north and west from the landing area as had been planned, the Nazi commander was able to concentrate his troops along the hills and deliver a series of attacks against the Allied lines. He succeeded in sealing the bridgehead and pinning down our forces for four months. Allied counter-attacks on the ground, continuous bombardments by the Allied air forces, and, with the improvement in weather, the resumption of unloading of supplies helped secure the lines of the bridgehead. By the same token, however, the turn of events meant the Allies could not carry out the original strategy of quickly smashing the Gustav line and, moving rapidly, seize the Italian capital.

During the week of crisis when forced evacuation was a distinct possibility, our unit was deployed: laying mines, hauling supplies, and strengthening our defenses. We maintained only one anti-aircraft position since German air attacks were infrequent, taking the form of low level sneak-in-and-run maneuvers. Our defensive position in the air was strengthened when we set up a landing strip that served a U.S. Air Force fighter group flown by African-American officers. We relaxed in the knowledge that most of the time the air over the beachhead was dominated by Allied planes.

The situation on the ground, however, was far different. The intensity of the German artillery attacks seemed to grow daily. During the critical days when we were threatened with evacuation we were busy enough with a variety of tasks to disregard the shelling. When our military situation had improved there was not a great deal to be done other than eat three meals a day, sleep when the neighborhood was quiet, and figure out how to stay out of harm's way. The Nazi gunners positioned on the Alban Hills actually made our calculations easier, administering their barrages in a very systematic way. Bombardments began at the start of breakfast. We countered with an easy solution: change the time for breakfast. Furthermore, over a given period of time the shells landed in clusters near each other, leading us to deduce that the guns had not been moved from one shelling to the next. Conventional wisdom (or was it an old wive's tale?) had it that shells fired successively from the same position would not land in the same spot (compare the saying that lightning does not strike twice in the same place). Artillery men near us mumbled something about deflections as the result of gun vibration. We did not want to be seen as stupid and did not expand our inquiry.

Whether these allegations were true or not did not seem to matter. We behaved as if they were. Some of us no doubt realized that for purposes of maintaining mental health, believing in something even if not true may be as beneficial as being guided by scientific facts. So at the start of a barrage we, or several of us, jumped into craters made by an earlier bombardment. It worked well for us. Hardly scientific proof but something to chew on.

In the course of time, the shelling eased up. We thought it was due to the placement of smoke pots all over the beachhead, a tactic which seriously interfered with the Nazi gunners' ability to observe the results of their shelling. It is also possible that our own relentless land and air bombardment resulted in a shortage of German ammunition. In preparation for a future breakout from the beachhead German-held areas beyond the Nazi line were now being targeted by the American strategic air force. The build-up of supplies for defense and future attack also continued with most beachhead areas beginning to take on a look of normalcy. This turn of events was best demonstrated by the arrival of a group of American Red Cross workers, most of whom were women. Happily, this reminded us that the almost total lack of females, except for nurses and a few local Italians who would not be moved, was only a temporary phenomenon.

What do GIs do when cooped up on a beachhead with little to do? How many interesting or enterprising ways can they find to get into trouble? On a trip to the town of Anzio we located a barrel of red wine in an abandoned house. We filled our canteens and nailed the doors shut so that nobody would take *our* wine away from us. The following night we returned, armed with two five-gallon cans. Upon returning to our dugouts we threw a little party with hospitality for friends nearby. In the middle of the night we woke up to a red alert indicating that enemy planes were headed our way. As members of an anti-aircraft battery we rushed to man the guns. I was particularly concerned about Gibson, our squad leader who had imbibed liberally the liquid stuff we had just brought home. My last glimpse of him indicated that he was desperately in need of a long stretch of sound sleep. It was all the more surprising that when I saw him, perhaps an hour after turning in, he was operating on all cylinders, giving orders in an assured, no-nonsense manner as becomes a non-commissioned officer.

In perhaps the third month of our stay at Anzio we began engaging in a larger extra-curricular project. Under Gibson's leadership we built a still. All the knowledge and skill for the project originated with him. He decided that the best raw material for the product would be provided by the fruitbars the army had been distributing at breakfast. Where Gibson was able to secure the hardware for the still in a war-torn environment, where nearly all civilians had fled, was beyond my grasp, but obtain it he did.

With the easing of German shelling of the beachhead, the army gave orders to bring back a bit of garrison culture, read "spit and polish." We began policing areas (translate as picking up cigarette butts), paying attention to the uniform, and had periodic inspections by higher-ups. What would we do with our still? Surely this was a violation of one or more army regulations, although none of us was able to cite chapter and verse.

The still had been placed in a relatively "secure" environment, a deep dugout whose entrances were reinforced by wooden blanks. Besides the still there were in the dugout some pieces of garden furniture designed to promote rest and relaxation in keeping with the consumption of our homemade brew. We knew that the inspection of our area would be carried out by a colonel whose stature was marked by substantially more than average height and weight. With that observation in mind we knew that the only way to protect our retreat was to narrow its entrances. After some discussion we decided, as an urgent night project, to block one entrance entirely with the aid of sandbags and to reduce the second by about one third thus posing a major challenge to the colonel's passage. Our scheme succeeded magnificently. After one good but hardly penetrating look at our Still Recreation Center, he decided to move on without any comment.

With the Nazi blockade of Anzio coming to an end we took account of our good fortune. A number of men in our unit were killed by enemy fire although no one in my squad was lost. When we abandoned the beachhead we left behind a vast American cemetery filled with newly dug graves. I myself had several close escapes, the most narrow one occurring when a piece of shrapnel hit my ammunition belt and detonated three bullets which missed my body but tore my clothes (I was later told that the chance of bullets being set off outside the gun barrel are quite remote).

Before our pullout from the beachhead we were bivouacked near a unit of the U.S. Signal Intelligence Service. I befriended some of their men and found they were looking for a replacement of a unit member who had lost his life after the Anzio landing. They thought that my knowledge of German would certainly make me a candidate. After I held an interview with their commanding officer he spoke with the captain of my battery. They decided to request my transfer. Because of the classified nature of the work of the SIS, the transfer, I was told, would have to be arranged through the War Department in Washington, D.C.

As it turned out the papers on my reassignment caught up with me about two weeks later at Civitavecchia, a town roughly forty miles northwest of Rome. Our unit had joined the Allied thrust up the Italian peninsula to catch up with the retreating Nazi divisions. Following the four months confinement on the beachhead we welcomed the move as a liberating activity, which was crowned by a day of sightseeing in newly occupied Rome. Our day off significantly coincided with the good news that a second European front had been established in Normandy. The day was, of course June 6, 1944.

The captain of my old unit provided me with a jeep and driver for the transfer to my new assignment. But locating the new unit was infinitely more complicated than getting the paperwork done. The location noted in the papers was Naples, the major American base and overrun by GIs both on duty and off on a well-deserved break from months in battle situations.

On the way to Naples we stayed overnight with a quartermaster detachment in one of Rome's suburbs. An air raid interrupted our night's sleep, but no bombs fell in our immediate vicinity, and we had no idea what was the intended target. Newly liberated Rome was still celebrating and air attacks by the depleted Luftwaffe seemed strangely out of place.

We reached Naples before noon on the following day and immediately began searching for the Signal Intelligence unit to which I had been assigned. I had to do it without a vehicle since my driver was obligated to return to his outfit. The afternoon search yielded no clues, but I discovered that the U.S. Army is a generous host to lost soldiers like myself and provides the most reliable bed and breakfast. To appease my slightly guilty conscience I reasoned that after four months of beachhead living, Uncle Sam owed me a few days off in civilized society.

Having convinced myself that my status was not AWOL (absence without leave) I decided to continue my hunt for my proper home by dividing the day into two: the morning devoted to continued efforts to locate my Signal Intelligence Service unit; the afternoon and evening set aside for sightseeing. Mount Vesuvius, having recently erupted, put on a special show for the visiting soldiers. Special, because eruptions have been rare in recent times and also because this one, being relatively minor, did not threaten nearby towns. An organized, army-sponsored tour took place at night when the fireworks emanating from the crater were more spectacular than during the day. Army trucks took us up the slopes but short of the area where the ground heat would have posed a threat to the tires. We proceeded on foot but turned back when the soles of our shoes became uncomfortably hot.

My unplanned holiday soon came to an end when an army officer from whom I sought information revealed that he had heard of the unit's location and offered to take me there. Upon arrival I realized why the unit was practically unknown. There were no signs guiding an outsider to the place. The SIS detachment was based in a Catholic monastery on a plateau overlooking the Bay of Naples. The spectacular view was framed by the resort of Sorrento and the islands of Capri and Ischia. A setting beyond compare. Monks and soldiers, I learned, enjoyed a peaceful co-existence. There was no crowding for space. The U.S. army provided the monks with drinking water brought in by a tank truck since the water line to the monastery had been cut. Individually, we shared some of our rations with the brothers and occasionally exchanged lessons in Italian and English. Our stay was clearly temporary and served the purpose of training in preparation for our roles in the next phase of the war.

Given the classified nature of the work I was about to do, I thought the Signal Intelligence Service people succeeded in camouflaging themselves and their activities. Up to this point I had only the vaguest idea of what was expected of me, but the secrecy surrounding the assignment gave it an aura of fascination and importance.

7

War from a Different Perspective

The task of the Signal Intelligence Service unit to which I had just been assigned was tracking enemy planes and providing our own air force with the information necessary to "down them" or use other means to put them out of action. In tuning in on bands of frequency used by the Luftwaffe, constantly searching the dials, we were able to interccpt the conversation among pilots or pilots and their ground stations. Two direction finders were used for triangulating the planes' location. Most voice interceptors also served as operators of the direction finders which went into action when enemy traffic (voice communication by Nazi pilots and/or ground stations) was picked up.

The unit, usually referred to as detachment, was headed by a captain and a lieutenant, the latter in charge of the voice interceptors. It also contained a crew of technicians skilled in setting up radio antennas, repairing electronic gear, providing transportation, and running the kitchen. The small size of the detachment and its physical isolation from other army units made for interdependence and informality. Since staffing was adequate, we could work in shifts which were handled flexibly, rotating everyone for duties during the day as well as at night. That was an appealing feature since it allowed operators to take a whole day off for sightseeing should they so wish.

The nature of the detachment's main task, interception of Luftwaffe traffic, put its stamp on the personnel. We all knew German. However, that qualification did not determine the personality or education of unit members. The lieutenant was born in the United States, had a Ph.D. in Germanic languages and was a professor of German at an American university. Another interceptor was German-born and taught economics at the college level. A third interceptor, though American-born, spoke a fluent German as a result of living with a German foster family. He was a conductor of a regional symphony orchestra in civilian life. Two members of the group studied German in college and had completed an army-sponsored program for translators. I myself was one of a group of four who had been brought up in Germany or Austria. Two of this group were in the midst of undergraduate studies when drafted; the other two were middle-aged and I don't remember the nature of their civilian occupations.

Of these two, one—whom we shall call Tony—stands out clearly in my mind. He spoke English with a heavy German accent and was the only American soldier known to me who was captured by American troops as a suspected spy. In fairness to Tony it should be mentioned that this happened during the campaign in the Rhineland when the Nazis promoted the infiltration of our lines by English-speaking soldiers in American uniforms. Tony came up with such droll statements as "I shpeak French, Tcherman, Italian, but English die best." Referring to our company dog named Sneaky he exclaimed, "When Sneaky hears die messkit klapper, he comes running."

My associates in the Signal Intelligence Service presented an interesting contrast to the men in the former unit, the airborne battery. The latter tended to accept their jobs and army life as a given and were not preoccupied with what could be, should be or might have been. There was little inclination to challenge basic beliefs or critique the mission of the army and the country. The men were keenly aware of their lack of power to influence events or to discuss how things could be done differently. There was consensus on everybody's most fervent wish: to get the war over with and return to civilian life.

I remember only three occasions of ideological encounters in units with which I was associated prior to this more permanent assignment. The first occurred in basic training in Alabama where there was an outbreak of anti-Semitism, giving rise to verbal and occasional physical conflict. The conflict was fed by the intense loyalty to the Vatican and sympathy for the Italian dictatorship of a group of Italian-American GIs, thrown into basic training with a group of New York Jews, plus a contingent of Southerners. A second occasion brought me into contact with a sailor of Russian descent on the LST with whom I discussed the compatibility of Soviet and western Allied goals in the post-war world. He was obviously concerned that the present war might not narrow the existing conflict between the two systems. The third occasion arose when a fellow soldier of Chicano background confessed to me in confidence that he had been a volunteer fighter in the Lincoln Brigade at the time of the Spanish Civil War and that he felt much less involved ideologically in the present war.

The men in the Signal Intelligence detachment were

also powerless, but, by virtue of their educational and occupational backgrounds felt a greater (albeit imaginary) sense of power that came to the fore when debating politics or military strategy. There were extensive discussions about our attitudes toward Germans who claim to have been anti-Nazi. Would we allow ourselves to be involved with German women? (We were still unaware of the army's non-fraternization laws, which were rarely enforced.) Should the Nazis' criminal upheaval change our attitudes toward German culture? The younger members of our group tended toward rejection of German people and culture which they saw intimately bound up with Naziism and anti-Semitism. The American-born lieutenant who taught German and older immigrants who had spent more time in pre-Nazi Germany were more prone to differentiate between German fascism and German culture.

When two or more members of the detachment got together in the operations room, mess hall, dorms or wherever, discussions were always in process about politics, music, experiences on leave, including short-term romances that merited reporting. There was also much discussion about post-war career plans, which, for the younger members, including myself, had not been formulated.

In August, 1944, our exceedingly pleasant stay at the monastery came to an end with orders to prepare for an invasion. Our detachment was split into several subgroups. My own assignment involved a transfer to the *Catoctin*, a passenger ship that served as the headquarters of the invading army. I was to serve under a British lieutenant in charge of the invasion fleet's intelligence service.

After a few days' cruising in the Mediterranean, our ship joined the rest of the flotilla assembled for Operation Dragoon, the Allied landing on August 15, on the south coast of France. This move was designed to relieve the pressure on Operation Overlord, launched on June 6th, on the beaches of Normandy. The U.S. and British troops were joined by Free French forces.

My assignment called for continued work on the *Catoctin* until notified to join my detachment on land secured by our troops. The landings were carried out against light resistance, and there was no hostile aerial activity during the first three of four days after the landings. Then perhaps on the fourth day, to the best of my recollection, at dusk, a sneak attack of low-flying German fighter planes took place aimed at the *Catoctin* and surrounding vessels unloading supplies. On that evening, contrary to my routine of previous days, I went from the evening meal—following my afternoon shift at the radio dial—directly to my bunk for a nap. I was awakened by a noise on the deck above me resembling pebbles dropped on the ship's hull. Within minutes, there was running in the corridors and shouting for medics. I lost no time running up a flight of stairs to the area where on previous days I had lingered on deck, relaxing in the cool evening air of the French Riviera.

What I encountered was a blood bath suffered by the sailors and soldiers who had gathered on deck on that evening. Our ship had sustained a direct hit from a number of cluster or anti-personnel bombs which do not penetrate steel plates but raise deadly havoc among people in the open in close proximity to each other. This was a surprise attack without prior warning. The voice interceptor did not detect hostile traffic and guns were not firing when the Nazi planes swooped across.

I was approached by a Jewish chaplain seeking information about victims of Jewish faith. I could not be helpful since I had not been on board very long and, though I had become acquainted with a few of the "evening crowd" hanging out on deck, I knew next to nothing about their private lives.

That invasion was over with little resistance, I rejoined my detachment. It felt good to be reunited with the men in the unit (they had set themselves up in a wooded area near Saint Tropez), and to be on French soil, closer to the Allied target of breaking the back of the Nazi war machine. At that point I also felt closer to the French than to the Italians because of some knowledge of the language and a previous visit, when younger, to their country. Several of my colleagues expressed their regret over my having missed the warm welcome and romance (read sexual adventures) which they had experienced in a newly liberated town. Returning to my unit signified return to a home of sorts where you find acceptance and support in difficult times. This is a recurrent theme among soldiers at war, particularly among those who constantly face injury or death.

As the Allies marched northward, aiming at the full liberation of France and the occupation of Nazi Germany, we set up our Signal Intelligence stations in forward positions at the maximum possible elevations. Fighters of the French Maquis, the underground army of freedom fighters that had been operating behind German lines in the Alpine region, advised us regarding locations. With a fluid front it was not always clear that our unit was operating in friendly territory and our efforts at camouflaging fell short of professional standards. On at least one occasion a German fighter plane overflew our position and waved at us, at least as confused regarding our whereabouts as we were.

During the subsequent weeks our detachment moved rapidly up the Rhone Valley and beyond, changing locations frequently until we reached the city of Nancy. In that vicinity there was a convergence of armies thrusting toward the German border from the north, west, and south. In Nancy we experienced a more settled existence; it felt good for a change to live in an urban setting with all the amenities of apartment living, a daily newspaper, concerts of classical music, and time off for sightseeing. In my case, there was time and opportunity for taking flute lessons.

The choice of flute lessons calls for some explanation. When I was a member of a Zionist youth group in Germany I learned to play an affordable musical instrument known as the recorder. My friends and I played simple classical pieces written for that instrument by Baroque composers such as Handel, Haydn, and Telemann. From that time on I had always wanted to play its big brother, a similar but larger instrument with a greater tonal range—namely, the flute. On entering a small French town shortly after its liberation by American troops, I discovered a music store. Its limited stock contained two or three flutes. An American infantry soldier who happened to be there, a man familiar with wind instruments, advised me on the best buy. Thus began a satisfying hobby, a non-career, an activity that has provided me with enormous pleasure to this day. I had my first lesson from a professeur de flute, a member of the Nancy symphony. Whether he accepted a beginner out of sympathy for the Yanks who helped liberate France or because of my ability to pay in C-rations, a commodity then worth more than French francs, I will never know.

Nancy offered the first opportunity to get to know French families. One of them, living near our apartment, asked me to escort their daughter to a subscription concert, a request that sprang from their belief that since the arrival of American troops, the city streets had become less safe for young women. Would they have defended their request by claiming that "some of their best friends are Americans?" None of the locals ventured the opinion that the streets were safer under Nazi occupation.

In making our way around the towns as well as others newly liberated, evidence of presumed collaboration with the Nazis emerged in the form of women whose heads were shaved by the Maquis. I personally was taken aback by occasional anti-Semitic remarks from the local population. I had to remind myself that France has a long anti-Jewish tradition (most cogently expressed in the Alfred Dreyfus affair) that preceded the collusion of Vichy with the Nazi occupiers. This took its most criminal form in the deportation of Jews to the death camps in Poland (my parents and many close relatives were among these victims). At the time this is being written (2003) the anti-Semitic movement is given new focus by attacks on synagogues and other Jewish institutions in various parts of France.

In the late fall of 1944, Allied armies were converging on Germany from both the east and the west. As the U.S. Seventh Army reached the Rhine in the Strasbourg area in late November, 1944, our unit was ordered to a forward position near that city. A rather cold winter was enveloping western Europe at that time and we had to equip ourselves for operating in the field. About a month later we were forced to retreat to the Nancy area as Hitler launched a counteroffensive in the Ardennes with the goal of disrupting the Allied front. American divisions, which took the brunt of the attack, and British as well as Canadian forces joined in some hard-fought battles to reestablish the lines and resume the drive to the Rhine and beyond, into the German heartland. When our detachment returned to Nancy some of our former neighbors confessed to having felt extreme anxiety over the possibility that the Nazis might return.

In March, 1945, military events moved toward a climax; there were several Rhine crossings by western Allied armies, and Soviet armies reached the gates of Berlin. As reported in chapter 5 our detachment crossed into Germany near Mannheim in late March, affording me an opportunity to visit my birthplace, and then headed east, taking up a variety of positions until the German surrender. In the face of the heavy domination of the skies by the Allied air forces, our interception tasks were minimal. On the morning of May 7th, while I was sitting by the switchboard, a call came in from headquarters stating that Germany had just signed the document of surrender to be effective May 9th. I lost no more than ten seconds to convey the thrilling news to the captain of our unit. His reply, delivered in an expressionless monotone was a "Roger, roger; thank you and out." What a response to one of the most significant pieces of information transmitted in my whole life! Some of the members of our technical crew, hearing the good news while digging a field latrine, knew how to seize the moment. They carved a plaque, naming the product of their efforts THE ADOLF HITLER MEMORIAL LATRINE. (Hitler had committed suicide on April 30.) There were some who argued that the title was an insult to all the good latrines in the world.

After May 7, the enormous administrative apparatus of our armed forces swung into action for redeployment on a worldwide scale of the men and women in uniform, The skies had turned friendly overnight and no one foresaw need for the type of signal intelligence we had practiced, at least not in the European theater of war. We did speculate, of course, on the possible reassignment to the Pacific where the war was still in high gear, and predictions as to its duration were useless. But, still and all, we were optimistic. The army's point system for discharge, based on an individual's past service, gave us a rough indication of how soon we would be eligible to return to civilian life.

Whether in war or peace it was clear to us that decisions on army life are made from the top down. Choice is certainly not part of the vocabulary. The men in our unit were reasonably relaxed about the future, believing that the system of discharge was probably a fair one and that their turn for returning home was not far off. There was a mild measure of regret over the breakup of the detachment because most members had been together for a long time (I was the last to join) and had a comfortable relationship with each other. But that sentiment was overshadowed by the strong desire to become civilians again.

I have no information about the disbanding of the detachment as I was one of the first to be reassigned. I do recall that within a very few days I found myself relocated, temporarily, to Bad Kissingen, a well-known German spa, roughly seventy miles east of Frankfurt. My new job required me to work in the American military government in Munich. What stands out most clearly in my memory about the stay at the resort was a concert for the troops by the world renown violinist, Jascha Heifetz. About a third of the audience were members of the British Army's Jewish Brigade. They were as starved for classical music as the rest of the audience, but they were more vocal in their wish to shape the program. The scheduled portion of the concert lasted a little over an hour, but at that point their clamour for encores shook the concert hall. Heifetz magnanimously obliged, and the responses to requests were only limited by the available sheet music for the accompanist. The sight of the great virtuoso who for yet another hour, with a deadpan expression, produced the most exquisite music, was unforgettable.

The remainder of our stay at the resort was mainly forgettable. I recall few details, and those that come to mind had little to do with taking the waters at the spa. A group of us, perhaps eight or ten, were brought together with orders for reassignment to military government in Munich. Everyone in the group spoke German, and perhaps half were German-born but not necessarily of Jewish origin. The travel orders called for a flight to Paris and travel by rail to Munich. We strained hard to understand the logic of this arrangement. We could have made far better time getting there on bicycles rather than flying first in the opposite direction and then using the slow —at that time— European rolling stock. We had, however, learned a long time ago that ours is not to reason why. On the flight to Paris arguments ensued on whether we should aim for the next train out of Paris and ultimately out of France or should we be more relaxed about the timetable (we had no clues regarding train schedules). The group was divided into two sub-groups: those who had a warm affinity for German culture and German environment and wanted to travel quickly and those who wished to keep a safe distance as long as possible. The lines were roughly drawn between non-Jewish and Jewish members of the group. I counted myself clearly among the latter. As a victim of Nazi persecution and, as I learned only much later, a survivor of what came to be known as the Holocaust and mass genocide of Jews, I needed some distance between most Germans and myself.

The group could reach no compromise regarding departure date, so I decided to make my own arrangements. I was determined to immerse myself in the sights and sounds of the French capital. Since this was only about ten months after liberation, U.S. soldiers could still benefit from feelings of gratitude from the French. The city was easily traveled. The Paris subway system, I discovered, was unique in the way the visitor can grasp quickly the scope of the network and the connections to be made between starting points and destinations of the traveler. Paris, liberated on August 25, 1944, had a feeling of normalcy. Over a period of a week I made my way from Notre Dame Cathedral to the Louvre, from a topless bar to the Paris Opera House.

Finally, feeling that the time had come to get back on track as a member of the U.S. Armed Forces, I went to the Paris Airport and had no problem arranging an immediate lift to Munich. I reported to the American officer in charge of personnel for military government services, located in the historic Rathaus (City Hall). He assigned me to a well-furnished apartment in a middle-class neighborhood where I shared quarters with three other GIs. It took several days for him to call me back. I could easily have explored more of the wonders of Paris without having been accused of dereliction of duty.

He had me observe the long lines of Germans who

turned up daily at the Rathaus with requests that needed approval from the military authorities. Those in line were screened by gatekeepers (German employees) who either referred them to a relevant department for action or had their requests denied. I was given only the vaguest guidelines regarding my role but encouraged to "fix the system if it does not work." I am not aware that I contributed substantially to the shortening of the lines, but I put my bilingual skills to work as best as I could in negotiations between the gatekeepers and the higher officials in military government. If our military had trained a cadre of officers to administer a collapsed society, they had not yet reported for duty. I found myself with much free time on my hands and enjoyed a sumptuous, daily mid-day dinner at the Rathaus restaurant to the accompaniment of live band music.

At some point the powers that be decided on a more formidable assignment for me, namely, an investigation of the financial networks of businesses with connections abroad. I don't recall whether my studies at the University of Minnesota had already included Economics 101. But, if it did, it would not have been of much help. The major who handed me the assignment was vague regarding a series of questions I put to him about the goals and methods of my new task. He also asked me whether I was interested in signing up for officers' training which doubtless included the obligation of extended service in the United States Army. My reply was "No thanks but thanks anyway; I am too eager to return to civilian life to learn to carry out investigations like the one you are asking me to do."

The less said about my new task the better. It was one of the most forgettable experiences in my life. There were no requests for submitting a plan, progress reports, periodic evaluations, a final document, etc. Am I the only one who feels guilty about accepting a job for which there is a lack of proper qualifications? I couldn't really reject it since at the lower echelons of a powerful bureaucracy, there are no provisions for a rejection. The new assignment carried with it perks, among which were a Mercedes and a German driver.

My undefined, unfinished job was happily cut short by a notification of a furlough granted so that I could visit my sister in England. Preceding this trip was an unusual, but serendipitous, visit to our Munich apartment by a middle-aged American woman who had spent the war years in Germany. She appeared to be a drifter, drawn to us by a desire to speak English. It was not clear to me whether she was caught by the war and found it too difficult to return or whether she deliberately chose to stay on. The lady was a romantic who was attracted by the life and architecture of medieval German towns. She was also a violinist who enjoyed playing her instrument on the streets in the middle of the night which earned her several arrests and referrals to mental hospitals. When I told her about my forthcoming trip to England she made a referral of her own with some desirable consequences.

One of her dear friends, she told me, worked at the American Embassy in London. They had not heard from each other since America entered the war and her friend, she thinks, does not even know whether she came through it alive. Would I phone her while there? As it turned out, her friend in London was not only delighted with the news but invited me and my sister to high tea at the Embassy garden. Her parting words were: "If you ever need any help with a visa" (we had told her that my sister was eager to join me in the States), "do feel free to contact me."

About a year after my discharge from the army I launched an effort to bring my sister Hedy to the United States. The delay in filing an application for her visa was the result of the inadvertent destruction of my citizenship papers (the reader will recall that I was naturalized in North Africa) when an inexperienced clerk at the discharge camp liquidated too many documents in my personal file. An SOS letter to the U.S. Immigration and Naturalization Service, requesting a duplicate copy of my naturalization certificate, and several follow-up messages met with zero response.

A tip from a friend suggested bypassing the bureaucracy and contacting U.S. Senator Ball of Minnesota (where I resided). This produced magic results. The INS branch in St. Paul contacted me urgently and I got my paper within two weeks.

This first successful lesson in cutting red tape led to a repeat performance, using informal channels to obtain a visa to the United States for Hedy. After there was a "routine delay" at the U.S. consulate in London, we remembered our friendly contact at the Embassy and discovered to our great delight that the eccentric violinist's friend was able to expedite Hedy's immigration considerably.

Upon arrival I immediately called my sister, who was working as a registered nurse at the Princess Elisabeth Children's Hospital in London. We had not seen each other since November, 1938, when I took Hedy to the train at the Mannheim Railroad Station, to join the Children's Transport to England. Her first words were "You sound so Yankee-like." She herself actually sounded more "Limey-like" than I did "Yankee-like" since she had lost all traces of a foreign accent. It was fortunate, nonetheless, that we spoke two versions of a language that resembled each other some of the time.

Hedy had more up-to-date information than I, albeit going back some three years, by virtue of the fact that she exchanged correspondence with our parents through relatives who lived in neutral Switzerland. The exchange took the form of our aunt Anna (my father's sister) forwarding mail from Hedy to my parents and vice-versa when our folks were still interned by the Vichy Government. The correspondence came to an end when my parents were deported to Auschwitz in August and September, 1942, respectively. The process of mass murder of Jews shipped from France started in March of that year and the Vichy Government collaborated in this phase of Nazi mass genocide. (It took till July 14, 2000 for the French Government to officially acknowledge collaboration and pay limited reparation to dependents who were under twenty-one years of age at the time their relatives were put on the trains to the death camps.)

At the time of our reunion Hedy and I had still hope for our parents' survival, and we pledged to pursue our inquiries as soon as we were free to explore the avenues for getting information. My first contact was with the mayor of Gurs near the central camp where our parents were first interned. The mayor replied that all camp inmates had been evacuated from Camp de Gurs and other camps in the area and transported east, presumably to Auschwitz. Details emerged only much later as the Klarsfelds (1983) documented the deportation of Jews from France.

Getting back to my army furlough in England, being reunited with Hedy, this was my first visit to that country. I was struck by the large number of GIs everywhere, indicating that the demobilization process and/or shifting of troops to the Pacific theater of war was not yet in high gear. The general impression gained was that with the European war at an end, we had begun to overstay our welcome in the British Isles.

A personal experience drove home that point. The British have an honorable tradition of observing lines or queues as a means of allotting goods or services on a equitable basis. This is particularly true when waiting one's turn for a ride on a train or bus, but queues are equally observed when buying goods in a store where there are more clients than sales personnel. A friend described to me a group of Londoners lining up outside a butcher shop in driving rain in order to preserve the just order of service inside the shop. During one of my travels around the city I made an effort to get on a bus that had just left its appointed stop. Being in a hurry to make it to a get-together on time, I ran after it and jumped on the rear platform as it gathered speed. The woman conductor dashed toward me and rang the bell to halt the vehicle, then pushed me off even before it had come to a full stop. The last words I heard when reaching the sidewalk had something to do with "these damn Yankees." As I looked back I realized that I had unintentionally short-circuited the line, jumping aboard when the bus had already departed from the stop, leaving behind two people whom she had declined to take aboard. So much for some extra courtesy to the men and women who helped avert a Nazi conquest of the British Isles.

It was during this visit to England that World War II came to an end with the unconditional surrender of Japan on August 14, 1945. V.J. Day (Victory over Japan) was officially celebrated the world over on August 15, and the center of London was the place to be if you happened to be in England. Hedy was working on the night of the 15th, but a close friend of hers, Ruth Goldstein, who had also come to England on the Children's Transport, joined me to get a taste of the merriments in the streets of the British capital. We joined over a million people who were jubilantly crowded into Trafalgar Square. After observing for maybe a couple of hours the most interesting and heartwarming scenes, we reached the limit of our endurance and felt the need to return to home base. The problem was that at eleven P.M. the underground (subways) stopped running as it had done since time immemorial. No concession for V.J. Day and the hundreds of thousands who found themselves stranded far from home. So Ruth and I started walking in the general direction of our respective quarters. Attempts at hailing cabs were uniformly futile. The time by now was more than an hour past midnight and the long walk loomed ahead. Suddenly a car stopped in front of us and offered unlicensed services to wherever we wished to go. There was no haggling over price, since we were quite ready to end an eventful day well before sunrise on the next one.

V.J. Day signaled for me the end of my nearly three-year (thirty-five month) army career. With the end of the fighting in the Pacific theater of war the American war machine moved forcefully into high gear, returning the men and women of the armed forces back into civilian life. Upon returning to Munich from my England furlough, I discovered to my great joy that the point system for discharge put me in a priority position for return to the United States and an early discharge.

Munich, its physical appeal notwithstanding, held no

attraction for me. I felt ill at ease being in a city where Hitler's beer-hall putsch gave rise to the most cruel and criminal regime in modern times. When meeting Germans at work or in the streets the question invariably popped into my mind: had they played a role in giving rise and perpetuating the Nazi regime of terror?

The return home by way of several staging areas in southern Germany and France proceeded at a slow pace, for there was a shortage of accommodations in land and sea transportation. In selected locations the boredom of GIs on the waiting list found expression in polluting the airwaves with crude sexual and scatological broadcasts. Television fortunately was not yet available. Packed Liberty ships, though infinitely faster than LSTs, seemed to move at a snail's pace. To boost good feelings and patience I had to remind myself of the difference in the two voyages: that two and a half years earlier at every moment of four weeks at sea our lives were at risk posed by German U-boats roaming the Atlantic.

On the 21st of October, 1945, I was handed my discharge papers at Camp McCoy, Wisconsin. It took me a moment to realize that they were a great gift that enabled me to take charge again of my own life. This was happening at a point in history when a grateful nation was extending its hands to the many veterans who had served their country and needed help in adjusting to civilian life.

8

The Screening of Post-War America — A View from the Campus

My return to civilian life was marked by reunions with the many friends I had acquired during the two-and-a half years in the Twin Cities before being drafted into the army. Closest, of course, was the Weiller family, Molly and her husband Henry, who had treated me like a son. Their own adopted son David, who was in his mid-twenties, spent more time away from home than in it. His life was punctuated by epilepsy with frequent grand mal attacks that prevented him from holding a job. Fortunately, the family was able to support him financially, but the relationship was characterized by frequent disagreements and lack of affection. As time went on new pharmaceuticals enabled him to live a more normal life. However, it was tragically cut short by a fatal car accident not connected with his medical condition.

Molly had been my most frequent and regular correspondent while I was overseas. Her letters were interspersed with packages that contained her trademark product, chocolate-filled prunes, which she prepared regularly as a money-raising project for Hadassah, the women's Zionist organization. One of her packages, containing this delicacy, was so well-wrapped that it survived an eight-month delay in being delivered on the Anzio beachhead.

The Weillers, being forever generous, offered to shelter me until I was able to get settled. My immediate goal was to resume studies at the University of Minnesota. This would be after the New Year holiday of 1946. Until then I had a chance to update my academic record by posting credits in public health (conferred automatically on GIs who had undergone basic training), French literature (based on a correspondence course taken overseas), and German (requiring the passing of written tests). As I recall this process netted me twelve credits or nearly a quarter's (corresponds to a trimester in other universities) worth of work.

My correspondence course in French was part of an overall plan to continue my formal education even while serving in the army. Basic training, as the reader will recall, was so demanding that it left little room for anything but struggling for physical survival. Sicily presented a different situation. Between the time of the invasion, which I missed, and the advance up the Italian peninsula we had more free time than our high command could plan for. It was then that I decided to sign up for a correspondence course in introductory physics (offered by the University of Minnesota) which would help to fulfill my science requirement for graduation. The course material arrived after we had settled on the Anzio beachhead. During one of the bombardments launched from the hills overlooking the beachhead, my barracks bag was hit by a projectile. The bag and contents evaporated, a sign from heaven that I was not meant for a career in science.

What a surprise when I ran into a problem in acquiring credits for German. The test, which included writing an essay, earned me a B+. I asked the professor scoring the test why he gave me a B+ rather than an A or A-. He replied that for a German with my background and level of education I should have done better. I expressed puzzlement over his way of judging a product relative to background rather than on its own merit. Students in the German department conjectured that his Nazi sympathies might have been the real reason for the grade. My essay dealing with wartime experiences was hardly designed to evoke applause from a person on the other side of the fence.

In putting together my curriculum of required and elective courses I reached the conclusion that graduation in two years was within reach. I was actually able to complete my Bachelor of Arts degree in eighteen months as a result of the financial support from the G.I. Bill of Rights.

At the time of my discharge from the army, financial planning was not on my agenda. During nearly three years of service Uncle Sam took care of my physical needs and even provided me with a term life insurance. That insurance could have been carried over into civilian life with a small annual premium, but due to my financial naïveté I dropped the plan. Anticipating a period of unemployment I signed up for the so-called "52/20 club" or unemployment for veterans which paid twenty dollars for fifty-two weeks. However, with GI Bill payments due to arrive after the start of the winter quarter, I was able to cancel my application for the unemployment insurance.

The GI Bill of Rights, also known as the Servicemen's Readjustment Act of 1944, was described by the Senate's Finance Committee as a "fundamental bill of rights to facilitate the return of service men and women into civilian life" (Axinn and Levin, 1975, pp. 232–233). Restoration to civilian status was to be facilitated by means of education and training, loans to purchase a business or farm, and employment services. For me the GI bill was the most significant assistance I received in pursuing an academic career. Payment of tuition and a cost-of-living allowance enabled me to pursue studies full-time and work part-time as the need arose. The campus of the University of Minnesota had become my favorite hang-out. Like myself, a number of my male friends had returned from the war to resume their studies while women I had known were more likely to have graduated and left the area. Hillel House, the Jewish Students' Foundation, was for me—as before the war—a place of welcoming faces and Jewish cultural activities. I joined the American Veterans Committee, the most liberal of veterans organizations, and was active in neighborhood caucuses before elections. I no longer sought affiliation with one of the Zionist youth movements whose goal was settlement in an agricultural *kibbutz* in Palestine (later Israel). My academic goals, interrupted by the war, now took center stage, expedited as they were by the financial support of the GI bill. Nonetheless, I still saw the likelihood of continued study and employment in the future Jewish state. The organization that at that point more readily represented my present goals for living in Israel was *Hechalutz* (Hebrew term for pioneer) which had a chapter in the Twin Cities. Its ideological framework was considerably more open-ended than that of the various Zionist youth movements that I had known in the past. Members of the Minnesota group were, for the most part, college students pursuing their studies at the undergraduate or post-baccalaureate level. Their sympathies tended more toward the Israeli labor parties than the middle-of-the-road Zionist factions. Only a few members of the Minnesota group envisaged collective living in an agricultural settlement.

My ties with the Zionist movement found a tangible expression in working during the summer season at Herzl Camp, a Zionist camp for young people sponsored by the Jewish Youth Commission of Minneapolis and Saint Paul. Theodore Herzl was a key figure in the genesis of the modern Jewish state and is generally considered the father of political Zionism. Herzl Camp, under the leadership of Walter Plaut, a rabbi associated with the American Union of Hebrew Congregations (better known as the Reform Movement in American Judaism), attempted to cultivate a sense of identity with Judaism and an appreciation of the Zionist idea as a key element in Jewish survival. It was an exciting time to be a Zionist, for there was special impetus generated by the founding of the Jewish state in 1948. The emergence of statehood in the face of an invasion by seven Arab armies and in the wake of the Nazi-driven Holocaust turned Zionism into a movement that had the support of the majority of world Jewry.

The summer season at Herzl was divided into three camp periods of three weeks, each cycle comprising successively older campers ranging in age from ten to eighteen. There was also a young adult period of one week for campers beyond high school. During three successive camp seasons, my role was counselor during the first, assistant camp director during the second and third, and director of the young adult week during the third as well.

A training period of one week preceded each season in the course of which the counselors helped with preparing the physical setting, engaged, under the leadership of Rabbi Plaut and his wife Hadassah, in discussing program, and participated in seminars led by guest lecturers, on the subjects of group work and Jewish culture.

The third year afforded me an opportunity to use camp as a setting for carrying out a sociological study, a requirement for the master's degree in sociology and psychology at the University of Minnesota. Upon graduation with a B.A. in 1947, I was accepted into the graduate program of the Department of Sociology. My plan at that stage of study was to complete work for the master's degree and apply for acceptance into the Ph.D. program at the Hebrew University.

It was no accident that as a subject of my dissertation I chose ethnic identification. The writings of the psychologist Kurt Lewin, who postulated a direct association between a sense of personal identity and social adjustment, served me as a theoretical basis for the research (Lewin, 1945, pp. 169–185; Geismar, 1954, pp. 33–60). Teaching part-time at an afternoon Hebrew school, the Talmud Torah of Minneapolis, provided me with a setting for developing a scale to measure Jewish identification.

The reader may well ask whether it is good social science practice to investigate issues on which the researcher has already taken a strong ideological position. At the time I was engaged in this project, sociologists were divided into at least two groups. The strict empiricists, including the Chairman of my Department, Professor Stuart F. Chapin, argued for maintaining a strict separation between personal beliefs and research in corresponding areas. But other sociologists held that good research methodology and personal integrity were sufficient safeguards against confusing ideology and research.

As I already indicated, an important objective of Herzl Camp was the strengthening of the campers' Jewish identity, and that goal was considered especially important for children living in small communities where Jewish peer groups and institutions were lacking. Not every observer of the Herzl program would necessarily agree with its goals. Among the guest lecturers who were invited to assist with the staff training was Gisella Konopka, a distinguished professor of Social Work at the University of Minnesota. Professor Konopka was of the opinion that the camp program represented a socialization process which she saw as being akin to brainwashing. The main shortcoming, she believed, resided in our failure to allow the campers to arrive at a program by way of a democratic process in which the campers played a major role. Staff participants, however, were skeptical that strong progams for children and youths could evolve in a cultural vacuum without a blueprint rooted in the basic ideas and values of the program leaders.

Without a doubt, Herzl Camp involved its subjects in an experience marked by emotional symbolism. An example of this may be found in a counselor's description below of a ceremony commemorating the destruction of the Jewish Temples in the years 580 B.C.E. and 70 C.E. The events are remembered annually on the fast day of Tisha B'Av or the ninth day of the month of *Av* (around August). Traditionally, this was observed as a day of fasting and prayer, an occasion for mourning the destroyed temples and the loss of the homeland. At camp we tried to re-evaluate the fast day in the light of the restoration of the Jewish state.

At supper, just before the fast day began (Jewish fast days begin at sundown) campers were told that a special program awaited them and that all talking must cease when the bugle call announces the beginning of the fast.

At the bugle call, all lights were turned out. Campers waited in pairs at the doors of their cabins until the figure of a runner appeared out of the dark. This was the signal for the start of the ceremony, and everyone walked silently toward the recreation hall. The large log cabin was a strange building that night. Candles sputtered on benches, and the darting shadows emphasized the mysterious atmosphere. Partners were separated and directed to a spot on the floor by the nod of an usher's head. Campers were seated on blankets, about five feet apart from each other to emphasize the solemnity of the occasion. The windows and doors were draped in black, and the stage was empty save for a candlestick atop a pile of black boxes.

When everyone was seated, a voice came out of the dark. It told the meaning of Tisha B'Av and led campers and counselors in reciting prayers from a program handed out prior to the ceremony. The prayers were not traditional ones. One was a poem by a medieval poet, Yehuda Halevi. Another was the haunting Biblical passage: "If I forget thee, O Jerusalem, may my right hand forget its cunning." The third was the prayer for strength uttered by a Jewish partisan during World War II. All of them lamented the loss of the state and of Jerusalem and deplored the fate of exile.

A moment of silence followed the prayers, when a black figure slowly made her way from the entrance to the stage, singing tenderly a melody filled with longing for Jerusalem. The singer symbolized centuries of Jewish suffering in exile and the age-old hope for return. She lit the lone candle on the stage, then slowly made her exit, walking to the door still singing.

The first voice began again with the description of the battle which raged around the Second Temple, and as it told of the torches setting fire to the walls of the Sanctuary, a miniature temple in the center of the hall burst into flames.

As all present stared at the embers of the dying fire, the call of the bugle sounded again. It was echoed by a second bugle from the far end of the camp. The bugle calls were followed by the proclamation: One thousand eight hundred and seventy-eight years later, on May 18, 1948, the State of Israel was reborn! The gloom of the evening yielded to a feeling of pride and self-confidence. The camp was unusually quiet that night. Few words were spoken as the campers returned to their cabins and went to bed.

The program of Herzl Camp included a daily schedule of small discussion groups that touched on many subjects often chosen by the campers, sports activities, arts and crafts, choral singing, Sabbath religious services, overnight hikes and campouts in tents at sites some distance from the eighty-acre regular area.

I found the research process in which I was engaged during the camp season a valuable and most enjoyable experience. Valuable, because it furnished me with a launching platform for a career in social research. Enjoyable, as I was able to integrate it with my work as a camp counselor/administrator, work which I relished, without arousing the ire of the research subjects. I was, in fact, pleasantly surprised at the amount of cooperation I received since I had been party to interviewing projects that presented countless barriers to successful research. Playing in my favor were the age of the campers (respondents were of high-school age), their availability over a three-week period, a discussion session on the use of social research, and the fact that I was an authority figure (Assistant Camp Director) whom they might have hesitated to displease.

The academic process surrounding my master's thesis carried a bag of surprises that a struggling graduate student does not anticipate. After accepting my proposal for the MA thesis my major advisor, Professor Clifford Kirkpatrick, left to become the chair of Sociology at the University of Indiana. His favorable comments on what I had been doing did not carry over to the remaining committee members. Professor Charles Bird of Psychology took over as head of the committee and, after reading my proposal, concluded I must be cracked to plan such a study unless I could come up with $10,000 to carry it out. Confronted by his incredulous assertion I replied that I did not have the resources to pony up even 5 percent of that amount.

In retrospect I must admit that at that early stage of my academic career I had not internalized a basic principle that underlies success in graduate study: Follow the professors' advice in general, display conformist behavior. I had enough sense, however, to avoid seeking the support of another committee member, an act that might have been fatal to my endeavor. Instead, I decided to plod ahead, counting on the assistance of fellow teachers and students at the Minneapolis Talmud Torah (where I taught part-time), the Herzl Camp Director, counselors, campers, and ultimately, my future wife.

Nearly two years later, I presented Dr. Bird with a draft of my thesis, hoping for the best. Less than a week passed when he sent a messenger to me while I was attending a graduate seminar, asking me to contact him at his office at my earliest convenience. Expecting the worst, I could not believe my ears when he said that after carefully reviewing my manuscript he was recommending it as a Ph.D. thesis. While at this point, admittedly, it was only his recommendation, I was not only very pleased but honored as well. Unfortunately, acting upon full committee support, which was not assured, would have meant radical changes in my life plans which, following marriage to Shirley Cooperman, had become "our" plans. We had completed all the arrangements for settling in Israel where I had already been accepted as a Ph.D. student at the Hebrew University. It seemed to make sense, therefore, to decline Professor Bird's offer.

The defense of what had now become a master's thesis, turned into a spectacle that I was unable to anticipate. Professor Theodore Caplow of the sociology faculty had taken over the committee chair from Professor Kirkpatrick. To bring the committee up to the required number of members, Professor George Vold, a criminologist, had been added.

Dr. Vold opened the defense with a statement to the effect that the work before the committee was a fine piece of research that was free of methodological problems but, all in all, represented a piece of work that could be described as "much to do about nothing. The problem Geismar is dealing with," I recall him saying is "the stubborn refusal of the Jewish people to assimilate into the larger society."

Wow, what a beginning! I was not aware that my thesis was meant to deal with the solution of the Jewish problem. What followed was a ninety-minute dialogue between Dr. Vold and myself without interruption from Dr. Caplow, the chair, or Dr. Bird. I no longer remember the details of the argument, but I fought back ideologically as best as I could. Although I was aware all along that my conduct could lead to a split among committee members on the merits of awarding me a degree, I was unable to steer the discussion toward the framework of my dissertation. It was Professor Bird who finally broke in: "This will lead us nowhere, and the time has come to send a gifted student on his way." Three days later, Professor Chapin, head of the Sociology Department, invited me to his office and congratulated me on completing the requirements for the master's degree and inviting me to become a candidate for the Ph.D. degree.

The transition from undergraduate to graduate some three years earlier had gone smoothly. Searching for a likely source of academic employment I went to the German department and discovered that they were looking for a teaching assistant. Their pre-condition for employment was a major in German, or at least a minor. I gave thought to the latter alternative but asked for time to make up my mind. My next stop was the newly formed Social Science department chaired by Professor Arthur Naftalin, co-founder with Senator Hubert Humphrey of the Americans for Democratic Action and later Mayor of Minneapolis. He offered me a quarter-time assistantship, and immediately I signed on the dotted line. A few days later the Sociology department came through with an offer for a half-time assistantship, which I accepted with delight. This put me in a position to decline the German Department assistantship and settle cheerfully for a three-quarter time appointment in the two social science entities.

Teaching assistants are at the bottom of the academic hierarchy and work at the pleasure of the senior faculty. Teaching assistants or T.A.s are expected to carry out routine tasks, their salaries are low, and they receive no fringe benefits or did not do so during the post-war era. There was no union protection for T.A.s at that time either.

Given all these deficits I expected to find myself in a less than satisfying situation, the academic label of the job notwithstanding. Quite to the contrary. Starting with income from the two assistantships combined with payments from the GI Bill left me, in my single status, without financial concerns. Both Professors Kirkpatrick and Naftalin were pleasant to work with, and I had no complaints about making up and scoring exam questions. Teaching recitation sections, small classes made up of students attending lectures given by senior professors, was, however, a challenge, for it was my first opportunity to test myself as a teacher in an academic setting.

The most remarkable and gratifying aspect of being a teaching or research assistant in the late 1940s at the University of Minnesota was the arrangement of work spaces. Assistants in the departments under the headings Science, Literature and the Arts were given desks on the top floor (referred to as the loft) in a building which, I believe, was known as Nicholson Hall. Most of the desks were placed in an open area, without partitions, allowing for intellectual and social interaction among the assistants. For many of us the loft was a place where we exchanged information about the University, discussed strategies of getting along and getting ahead, debated political orientations, or just spent time relaxing over a cup of coffee drawn from a kettle that was kept warm all day.

The loft was a home away from home. Graduate assistants who tired from doing their work would take time off to have lunch or just a cup of coffee together or go for a walk. On weekends, a small group might gather for an informal party, chamber music, or group singing. The Loft atmosphere tended to attract some more senior faculty members to the cross-discipline ambiance and sociability of the place. After an academic career with appointments at the junior and senior levels I can fully appreciate the selective advantages—though overshadowed by drawbacks in income and security—of junior academic status. Without the same need to defend one's turf and demonstrate advanced competence there is among junior staff more intellectual openness toward the process and structure of knowledge development.

The sociology contingent of the assistants with whom I was closely associated had a number of political activists, who, like myself, had served in the U.S. Army during and following World War II. We had in common membership in the American Veterans Committee, whose political ideology favored social reform and detente with the Soviet Union. In the upcoming presidential elections in November 1948, the leading candidates were President Harry S. Truman (Democrat) and Thomas E. Dewey (Republican). As a group we clearly favored President Truman for his progressive social policy but had serious reservations regarding his hawkish attitudes toward the Soviet Union. In balance the group's overriding concern was survival in a world threatened by nuclear war (President Truman announced in September that the Soviet Union had developed an atomic bomb).

Given the foregoing considerations our group favored in the 1948 elections neither major candidate but encouraged voting for the head of the newly formed Progressive Party, former Vice President Henry A. Wallace. Wallace had substantial support from the political left including the Communist Party, a fact which concerned most of our group, but a major consideration in our choice was the strong lead of Dewey in the public opinion polls, seemingly putting a Truman victory out of reach. (As sociologists we had a fair amount of trust in polls which, we found out later, was hardly justified.)

Candidates of independent or minority parties are not known for winning presidential elections. They are, however, in a position to alter the outcome when the margin of votes for either major candidates is small. With the seeming likelihood of a Dewey sweep a strong Wallace endorsement would signify a casting of our ballots for the best candidate and also register a strong protest vote.

A $10,000 contribution to the Wallace campaign from Dimitri Mitropoulos, then music director of the Minneapolis Symphony (now known as the Minnesota Orchestra), provided the volunteer groups at the University of Minnesota with funds to produce and distribute pamphlets and campaign buttons. The sociologist activists among the teaching assistants, including myself, attended neighborhood primaries, made speeches to whoever was willing to listen and wore Wallace buttons. Professor Chapin, head of the Sociology Department, let it be known that he disapproved of our habit of wearing campaign buttons while teaching class but did not interfere with our practice.

I spent the summer of 1948 away from the university campus as assistant director of Herzl Camp. This was also the summer when I moved a step closer to ending my bachelor existence. A First of May party was held at the home of my landlady who rented rooms to students in the campus vicinity. Her children, members of the left-wing Zionist youth movement, *Hashomer Hatzair*, hosted a party whose theme was celebrating May 1, as the international workers's holiday. Most of those attending, about a dozen in number, were members of the organization. The three or four non-members who were there were judged to be ideologically sympathetic to the organization or had a potential for membership. The young woman in whom I developed a strong interest, Shirley Cooperman—belonged to the latter category.

We met often over the following few weeks giving rise to a blossoming relationship whose development, I feared, would have to be put on hold because of my commitment to Herzl Camp. (The travel distance from camp to the Twin Cities was about three hours by car, which neither of us had, and longer by train.) Continuity of the relationship called for a more daring plan taking the form of requesting an appointment for Shirley as a counselor at Herzl Camp. Rabbi Plaut was most obliging when I visited him for a planning session in Fargo, North Dakota, where he headed a congregation. He informed me that he was ready to hire Shirley "sight unseen." The rest is history.

We set our marriage date for September 19, 1948, one week before the start of the fall quarter (trimester) at the university. The starting date affected both of us significantly. Shirley started classes as a freshman at the University of Minnesota, I resumed my duties as a teaching assistant in Sociology. That left us less than a week for a honeymoon on the north shore of Lake Superior.

The atmosphere on the campus of the University of Minnesota in the late 1940s was one of optimism and confidence in the future. World War II had ended, students in large numbers were either resuming or beginning their studies with financial support from the government, and positions were opening up to accommodate their educational needs. McCarthyism, the witch hunt for communists and other left-leaning individuals (named after Senator Joseph McCarthy who led and embodied the campaign to eradicate such influences in government and public life), was just beginning to raise its ugly head. McCarthyism was hardly original in its goals. It was able to build on the work of the House Un-American Activities Committee. But its methods using hearsay, innuendo, and repressive measures leading to a loss of livelihood, were unique in modern American society (their use eventually led to the demise of the senator, following congressional censure, after he took it upon himself to smear the American military).

In the growing Cold War climate, beliefs favoring reform, social change, or any mode of socialism were met with a good deal of suspicion in this country. The suspicion was reinforced at the highest level of government by men like J. Edgar Hoover, head of the Federal Bureau of Investigation from 1924 to 1972, who used harassment as a means of dealing with dissenters. While the principle of academic freedom is meant to bestow on faculty an unchallenged right for individuals to express themselves on any subject without fear of negative consequences, the reality is sometimes out of line with this principle as we learned during the McCarthy era.

A faculty member can't help being aware of situations that pose potential controversy. I recall that in one of my classes where I discussed social science theories of the nineteenth century I became self-conscious about having an FBI agent among my students. Since he was a regular college student and volunteered the information about his employment, his class attendance was probably free of ulterior motives. Still and all, when discussing Marxism, I watched his facial expressions trying to read his reactions. He seemed to nod assent, meaning he understood what I was saying with regard to all the theories including those of Karl Marx.

The time was short from the start of classes to election day in November, 1948. As a teaching assistant I was preoccupied with both taking and teaching new classes. The latter typically was a recitation section of a course taught by a professor. Recitation sections in contrast to the lecture, whose attendance could reach three hundred, were limited to twenty-five or thirty students.

Among the graduate students hanging out at the loft at Nicholson Hall, election activity was at a low ebb, probably due to the fact that the polls were predicting Dewey the highly probable winner. On election night my wife and I were listening to election returns until some time after midnight the Wednesday edition of the *Chicago Tribune* announced Dewey the thirty-third president of the United States of America. When Shirley and I awoke the following morning in time to catch the bus to campus, we learned that President Truman had in fact amassed enough popular and electoral votes to be the unquestionable winner. My personal reaction was "I should kick myself very hard," considering the possibility that my vote might well have helped put Governor Dewey in the White House. The failure of the polls to make a more accurate prediction gave rise to countless studies and eventually to significant improvements in the methodology of opinion polling.

1948 was also the year when the Jewish State of Israel came into being. It happened on May 14, in the wake of United Nations votes by the Security Council and the

General Assembly to partition Palestine into Jewish and Arab states. The Arab's immediate response was an attempt to conquer the whole area that constituted the former British Mandate. Five armies of the countries associated with the Arab League started the invasion of the land awarded to the Jews.

The sympathies expressed on campus, as in much of the country, strongly favored the Jewish cause. In the face of ever-growing evidence of the destruction of Jewish life in Nazi-controlled areas of Europe, there was overwhelming support for a Jewish homeland on territory connected with the Jewish past. A number of Jewish students I met expressed an interest in signing up with the Israeli armed forces to defend the newly created state.

Unlike the German Jewish community during the Weimar Republic, American Jews were not widely split on the issue of Zionism. The American Council of Judaism was one of the few organizations that opposed Zionism and maintained that Judaism is a religion, not a nationality. Its influence in the American Jewish community was limited. Non-supporters of the idea of a Jewish state were more typically people lacking interest in the subject than ideological opponents. Events at the United Nations and in the Middle East, coming in the wake of the Holocaust, generated a strong rally of American Jewry on behalf of the Jewish state.

In the months following our wedding, Shirley and I were seriously thinking about settling in Israel after I completed the master's program. During the intervening two years, we lived in a room with housekeeping privileges in an area of Minneapolis with easy public transportation access to the campus. We both took classes, Shirley with a major in English and art and I in graduate studies in sociology. Furthermore, I did research on my master's thesis and held a three quarter-time assistantship in sociology and social science. Shirley had a paid position as an organizer of Young Judea (Zionist) youth groups in Minneapolis and as a song leader in the Minneapolis Talmud Torah. G.I. Bill support supplemented by the part-time jobs added up to a modest budget that allowed for the rental of a flea-bitten, mice-infested apartment (we eventually convinced the landlady to bring in an exterminator after being kept awake at night by traps going off). The budget took into account the need to put aside some money for our planned resettlement in Israel.

The first two years of marriage added up to a busy schedule of study, work, and efforts to prepare ourselves for living in a different culture with a different language. Our preparation was in part ideological, meaning to firm up our conviction that the State of Israel is a key element in Jewish survival and that by settling there we would make a contribution to its existence. It was after all Ben Gurion, the first prime minister, who made an appeal to Jews from Western countries, the United States included, to bring their special skills and education to bear on the historic endeavor. We were, indeed, looking forward to becoming witnesses to the birth of a Jewish state in modern times.

Up to this point our preparation for using Hebrew, the official language of Israel, was quite limited. We had both studied Hebrew as teenagers in Hebrew school. The emphasis had been on reciting prayers in synagogue and in the home celebration of the Sabbath and holidays. Beyond that we had also picked up some Hebrew by way of learning songs, both religious and secular.

During the 1948–49 school year a petition made the rounds at the University of Minnesota requesting that Hebrew be a subject offered in the undergraduate curriculum. The petition was signed mainly, but not exclusively, by Jewish students who were interested in learning Hebrew as a living language. I asked for a meeting with the dean responsible for curriculum in the department of Science, Literature and Arts. The dean indicated to me his support in principle for offering Hebrew but also explained that it would have to be presented within a framework of academic linguistics. He elaborated that point by saying that he would eschew offering single courses in any language. Instead, the goal would be to teach Hebrew or any other foreign language within a structure that builds on the fundamentals of teaching a language and ultimately integrate it into a department of related languages.

Curriculum decisions in universities are not shaped by student petitions. The Science, Literature, and Arts program did, indeed, schedule a three-credit course in Hebrew, but the contents did not call for teaching it as a living language. The University hired a linguist, Dr. Pearson, who taught the fundamentals, which comprised learning the alphabet, pronunciation, and grammar. He had a Ph.D. in linguistics, and his religious orientation was Southern Baptist. Despite his engaging personality and liberal religious views he was the wrong person to teach the course. He did not speak Hebrew, and was unfamiliar with the modern idiom spoken in Israel. Most of the students who had signed the petition already knew how to read. Some could carry on a simple conversation.

When Shirley and I came to the first meeting of the class we realized that none of the petition signers had made an appearance. In fact, other than Shirley and myself there was a third Jewish student who, like ourselves, wished to improve his facility in reading and conversation. The remaining students in the class, three in all, wished to take the class to fulfill a requirement for the study of theology. Shirley and I, though we realized immediately that what Dr. Pearson had to offer was not what we were looking for, decided to remain registered and attend the class in order to support the idea of a Hebrew program at the University of Minnesota.

A more effective way of preparing for the impending migration to Israel included taking Hebrew courses for adults offered by the Hebrew schools in the Twin Cities and participation in the aforementioned organization called *Hechalutz* (Pioneers).

Did our preparation for life in Israel lead us to generate a realistic picture of what to anticipate after disembarking in Haifa harbor? The images that come to mind from films that we had seen about Jewish Palestine were young people dancing the *Horrah* (circle dance) after work in the fields until the late hours of the night and singing songs and reciting poetry on Sabbath afternoons. Since we were not preparing to join the real "pioneers" in their "conquest of labor," (a phrase denoting the process of turning farming, construction, and manufacturing into occupations pursued by Jews, unlike the situation prevailing in the Diaspora) but were planning to live in a city, Jerusalem, the idealized picture of Kibbutz life had no relevance for us.

We knew little about urban living in Israel but were aware of the scarcity of affordable housing and food rationing, particularly meat, chicken, eggs and milk. We anticipated a lower standard of living for ourselves than we enjoyed in the United States but viewed this not as hardship but rather a minor adjustment given the fact that during the first two years of our marriage our standard of living was modest by American middle-class criteria.

Learning a new language, Hebrew, would pose some challenges, but living in a country whose doors were wide open to immigrants would create a climate of acceptance of people who were making concerted efforts to acquire the linguistic skills necessary for work and social life. All in all, whatever reservations we had regarding our life in Israel were overshadowed by a sense of adventure and a belief that our going to Israel and possibly settling there for life would be the fulfillment of an obligation to the Jewish State, established after nearly two millenia of Diaspora.

9

Life in the Young Jewish State

The physical preparations for settlement in Israel were infinitely more complicated than those that were psychological and cultural. We felt, after all, quite at ease with the ideological underpinnings for *Aliya* (a Hebrew term meaning ascending to the land). By contrast, the physical arrangements were difficult, contingent upon knowledge of living conditions there and specifics about available housing as well as the clothing required in a different climate and social milieu. Coming directly from student life, we had few financial resources for this move. Still and all, we decided to splurge a bit, the rationale being that items we assumed we would need would be much more expensive when bought in Israel than in the U. S. And so we acquired a radio, a record player, and an antiquated refrigerator. Because we were coming as immigrants or potential long-term residents, Israeli customs allowed us to bring personal belongings into the country duty-free. Our prize import was a used Dodge station wagon. To ensure the use of the car for touring the country, we possessed a *Carnet de Passage*, an international license issued by the American Automobile Association to its members, which we had acquired in Minnesota before setting out on our journey.

It soon became clear that with this purchase and

import we had over-reached ourselves. The *Carnet* was clearly a document for tourists, not immigrants or long-term residents. The juxtaposition of the two, while not illegal, was incompatible. It aroused the suspicion of customs authorities who became convinced that we had brought in the vehicle tax-free for eventual sale, a clear violation of the law. We never had an explicit plan on what to do with the car other than tour the country. While Shirley and I cleared the customs in minutes, the station wagon was held for several days, adding to our anxiety and consternation in this new country where we had to immediately begin making arrangements for housing, jobs and graduate schooling.

There was an interesting prelude to the acquisition of the *Carnet de Passage*. We did not hold membership in the American Automobile Association since this was the first car we owned, but we wished to join in order to obtain the *Carnet* and the other available benefits such as emergency roadside help. However, there was one hitch, a formidable one, to our plan. The Minneapolis branch owned a country club reserved for the exclusive use of its members. You could join only by passing an admissions process that included a home visit by the organization's representative. Word was out that Jews were routinely refused membership and while the reasons were not disclosed, they were not hard to guess.

At the time Shirley and I applied for membership in the spring of 1948, members of the Jewish community in Minneapolis had already decided to break the ban, using legal processes if necessary. While we were not in on the deliberations preceding the action, we found ourselves among a small group of Jews, one that included the local rabbi, applying for membership. A scheduled visit to our apartment was made by a member of the Association. Shirley and I awaited his appearance with considerable apprehension, wondering whether our residence in this run-down, two-room flat would be seen as justification for disqualifying us from the rarified atmosphere of a Minnesota country club.

The visit turned out to be relaxed and indeed quite pleasant, with no intrusive or offensive questions. The reviewer took in the rather squalid surroundings without the flutter of an eyelash. We came to the conclusion that he realized he was dealing with students just starting out in life, and it certainly did no harm to let him know that we were emigrating, unlikely to enter the club's hallowed halls. Perhaps those on high in the organization had already decided to avert legal action by accepting Jewish applicants. At any rate, our application led to membership, and as far as we knew, other Jews were also accepted. Needless to say, Shirley and I never visited the AAA country club, and to this day, we don't know what we missed.

At the other end of our auto-ownership career were the problems the Carnet created for the Israeli police. Even fifty or more years ago Israel was a beleaguered state, and identity checks as a means of reducing terror attacks were common. The police patrolling the highways were, by and large, unfamiliar with the international license. Whenever stopped for identification, questions and arguments ensued, and we soon learned that it was best for us to pretend total ignorance of Hebrew. More often than not, the young troopers who were usually recent Iraqi immigrants, knowing little or no English, gave up, and let us proceed.

A few months later, after having used the car to

explore the country, we decided to get rid of it for we needed cash with a new baby coming. In this highly regulated, bureaucratic economy we were required to acquire an official permit, a measure by which the government attempted to control the black market. A high official at the Ministry of the Treasury (where Shirley worked as an English secretary) hearing of our car, intervened on our behalf to obtain the document. The sale price was regulated (it would have to be at or below the Israeli market value, a somewhat fictitious sum) and the purchaser was to be chosen by the Treasury. The buyer turned out to be a Regional Council office, an administrative branch of the Israeli Government. The dealings took many weeks to conclude, accompanied by entreaties to hurry matters along and also some misgivings on our part. Had we done the right thing? Others with such assets managed to wheel and deal much more successfully than we did. But the deal was eventually finalized, legally. Several weeks after delivering the car, the newspaper reported that a Dodge station wagon owned by the Regional Council was involved in a road accident and had overturned. There was no report on casualties or the car's condition. We knew from experience it would take a major calamity to up-end it, and wondered whether it could be repaired. How ironic that this vehicle would suffer damage so soon after leaving our hands.

But episodes in Israel with the car were in the future. In the U.S. prior to embarking on *Aliya*, we made a cross-country journey from Minnesota to New York, visiting with a friend from University of Minnesota days, Eddie Sturm, who lived in Brooklyn, allowing us a few days to explore the Big Apple. We then set sail for Israel on the SS *LaGuardia,* one of the passenger vessels still plying the Atlantic after WW II. Accommodations on the ship were modest, quite in keeping with our lifestyle. We could afford only dormitory-mode cabins, separate quarters for the sexes in the bottom tier of cabins. Tourist-class passengers, by far the majority of travelers on board, were allocated no more than a third of the ship's space.

Among our fellow passengers there were a number of young American Jews going to Israel not as tourists but, like ourselves, as prospective settlers. A sub-set of these appeared to have a reason for *Aliyah* far different from ours—not pioneering but escape from McCarthyism. A few of these had advanced degrees from top-rated universities and in one form or another had been exposed to the pressures exerted by the witch hunt that spread through academia and government offices. Our judgment regarding motives for going to Israel were, of course, inferential, but as a group these passengers lacked a background in Judaism and/or Zionist involvement, and some stated openly that their political background disqualified them for professional careers in the United States.

After an uneventful voyage we disembarked at the port of Haifa in September 1950, two days before Yom Kippur. As many readers will know, this is the most sacred of Jewish holidays observed by fasting and all-day prayer in the synagogue. The timing of our docking brought about many delays in getting possessions, and in particular the car, released from customs. Before going on to Jerusalem, which was to be our permanent home, we visited with the Stahl family, friends from the German Jewish youth movement, who had settled in a Haifa suburb, Tivon. In the dry climate of the Middle East, the town was known as a garden city, sporting many freestanding houses surrounded by open planted areas. What surprised us greatly when rising in the morning of Yom Kippur was the sight of many of our neighbors working in their gardens or relaxing under shade trees rather than attending services at a synagogue. This was our first inkling of what we found to be true at that time: the secularization of the vast majority of Israeli Jews.

We learned soon enough, however, that even though Israeli society was predominantly secular, the Tivon social landscape displayed to us on the high holidays was not the norm throughout the country. The manner of religious observance varied in keeping with the composition of communities and their accustomed ways of dealing with religion. Jerusalem, which was to be our final destination, certainly presented a very different picture for it contained within its borders districts like Mayah Shearim that are densely populated by ultra-orthodox Jews for whom strict religious conformity is a way of life.

When I felt that I had regained my land legs after nearly two weeks on the ocean, I headed for Jerusalem where the Hebrew University was situated. My goal was to locate housing, begin the search for a job, and also register for the Ph.D. program at the Hebrew University. Shirley stayed behind in Tivon with the Stahls, learning the ins and outs of food rationing and house tending, Israeli-style, with little available water.

In the late summer of 1950 Jerusalem was a divided city. The 1948 War of Independence, following in the wake of the United Nations General Assembly vote to partition Palestine, gave rise to two separate Jerusalem communities: The New City, in the hands of Israel, served as the capital of the Jewish state; The Old City, part of the Arab West Bank and administered by the Kingdom of Jordan, contained a large number of Palestinian Arabs who had fled the country during the fighting.

This was my first visit to Jerusalem, and I eagerly awaited catching a first glimpse of the place held sacred by Jews, Muslims, and Christians, the city designated by the United Nations for international status. The road ascending from the coastal plain still showed marks of the fierce battles for Jerusalem between Arabs and Jews for many abandoned, rusted army vehicles littered the side of the highway. In the late summer of 1950, the traveler ascending to Jerusalem traversed rounded mountaintops of brown and grey, a mountainous desert environment lacking greenery that was interspersed in places with the trees and cultivated fields of a few Jewish settlements like Kiryat Anavim.

The New City of Jerusalem was a bustling place (the Old City was definitely off limits to Israelis in 1950). Following the government's proclamation in 1949 that Jerusalem was to be the national capital, ministries formerly located in Tel Aviv were moving to Jerusalem as fast as arrangements could be made to transfer personnel and acquire space to begin operations there.

Friends living in Jerusalem graciously offered to house me while I made efforts to find a place to live and search for a job. Because of the strict rationing at that time and lacking the food stamps to contribute to the household, I shared only their breakfasts and took my own meals in town, meals consisting mostly of a *falafel* (a chickpea quennelle in a pita sandwich) and *gazoz* (a carbonated drink comparable to American soda pop). These were sold widely on the streets of Israel during the early days of the state. The problem with the gazoz, the sweet thirst quencher, was its being sold under the most unhygienic conditions. The customary way of cleaning glasses after their use by a customer was spraying them with cold water. While local *gazoz* drinkers had no doubt become immune to bacteria that survived the rudimentary cleansing, I had developed little or no immunity and came down with a strong case of diarrhea (the Hebrew word is *shilshul*, much more onomatopoetic) that kept me off the streets for two days. When I was finally able to continue the search, I found two rooms that were part of a family dwelling in a near western suburb, close to the friends whose hospitality I was enjoying. A garden shaded by date palms surrounded the large stone building and formed an extremely attractive setting. When Shirley and I moved our belongings to this first of our Israeli homes, we were unaware of the problems it would soon present.

The only memorable feature of that first moving process was the unloading. All our worldly goods were in two large lifts, or wooden crates used for sea voyage. Two husky Kurdish Jews (recognizable from their costumes, kerchiefs wound around their heads and harem-like pants) did the right thing by unpacking the crates to facilitate removing their contents. But then they tended to drop items off the back of the truck in order to save time. Among the items disposed of in this manner was the small refrigerator bought just days before departing New York. It literally bounced as it hit the ground. The end of the unloading was marked by a trumpeting announcement by one of the moving men who shouted with a thunderous voice, "And now, *baksheesh*" (tip or gratuity). We were left to haul the items dropped on the ground in the garden into our quarters, many feet away, the best way we could.

Soon the problem with our newly rented apartment

was revealed to us by an upstairs neighbor with whom we shared a bathroom. She asked us whether we knew that our apartment was below ground level and that it flooded every winter, following the heavy seasonal rains. Of course we had not known; winter would soon be upon us; we looked for signs of water stains but none could be found. Within a week after moving in, however, her warning proved to be more than justified.

The rainy season started early that year with a couple of moderately heavy downpours but we felt safe since there was nothing approximating torrential rains. Then it came. In the middle of the night we heard the sound of water dripping, and soon water began accumulating to a depth of about three or four inches all over the floors of our two rooms. Of course, our land lady had never mentioned the problem even though it had existed as far back as neighbors could remember. Nor was there any indication of past efforts to remedy the problem. We obviously were facing an emergency and had to get out of the place immediately. The landlady offered neither help nor advice and shrugged her shoulder as if to say, well, that's the way it is.

This time, our friends the Guttmans came to our rescue. Louis, a well-known sociologist and statistician whom I had first met on the Minneapolis Zionist scene, lived with his family not far from where we had been stranded. We followed their advice which was to take whatever we could move quickly by car and put the remainder on high ground until we could find a permanent place. In the interim period we accepted their invitation to stay with them.

The new search yielded a room with kitchen privileges in the suburb called Bayit V'Gan, in a building located across the road from the Mount Herzl Cemetery. This is the burial ground of Theodore Herzl, the father of political Zionism, of other leading personalities in the history of the Jewish state, and of soldiers who died in the country's wars. It was up the mountain road from our now sodden rooms, one of the apartments in a moderately sized brick building abutting a large field of nettles and weeds. While the setting left much to be desired it was on a bus route and, since it was on the second floor, was impervious to winter rains.

The woman from whom we rented the room did so, we later learned, mainly because we owned a refrigerator which she could share and which her household lacked. When she discovered its small dimensions she expressed her deep disappointment about the whole rental arrangement. "What a *pitzkeleh*" (Yiddish for tiny)," she lamented. That, however, was the least of our problems. Our first child, Layah, was born shortly after moving in. With a birthweight of less than five pounds, suffering from colic, and occupying a room adjacent to the landlord, her crying interfered with his sleeping schedule since he rose at three AM to pursue his trade of baker. Shirley did all she could to pacify the infant and finally held her on her own stomach for much of the night, which seemed to soothe and comfort her.

Housing thus presented us with problems we had not anticipated. Other physical aspects such as the program of food rationing we were able to take in our stride. The near complete absence of meat and chicken created no hardship since fish was available at least once a week and, luckier than most, our U.S. family often sent us care packages, containing precious coffee, dehydrated eggs and tins of tuna fish. A dozen ways of preparing eggplant became a challenge to the cook to break the dull routine of the restricted diet, and Shirley rose to the challenge resourcefully and imaginatively. More disturbing was our observation that a segment of the population succeeded in bypassing the rules and regulations of the government. Our landlady found a way to get milk, eggs and meat through private, illegal channels, storing them in our refrigerator. What irritated us particularly was her garnering extra portions for two middle-aged people whereas our family that now included a baby had to settle for much less.

That was just one of the examples that led us to realize the role that the phenomenon called "*protectsia*" played in Israeli life. Freely translated *protectsia* means nepotism. In behavioral terms *protectsia* means circumventing legal and ethical channels of conduct to achieve goals that benefit an individual, a family or a special interest group, and not the community at large. Those who gain from *protectsia* usually do so at the expense of others. When somebody gets more than their share of rationed food, others are shortchanged. Those who, because of special connections, manage to get served ahead of others at a doctor's office or a queue at a ticket office are putting others at a disadvantage.

There is probably not a country in the world where such conduct is unknown. But in much of western society, nepotism is practiced in a clandestine manner and officially condemned or, at the very least, frowned upon. In Israel, although *protectsia* was not considered desirable behavior, it was engaged in widely to the point where most persons had a story to tell about themselves or friends having taken advantage of situations involving patronage based on special relationships.

I had my own personal bout with the *protectsia* phenomenon when applying for a professional position, and the encounter was an important learning process for political survival in a bureaucratic system. The experience will be described later in this chapter.

Newcomers to Israel like Shirley and myself are usually too busy at first to take note of the political system in which they find themselves. As stated earlier, we were attracted by the opportunity to be part of an important historic event, the rebirth of the Jewish state after a hiatus of nearly two thousand years of dispersion or Diaspora.

Our first expression of dismay about the politics of Israel had to do with the fact that despite the secular majority of the population, the influence of religion was all pervasive and placed the country on the border of a theocracy. Public transportation came to a standstill on the Sabbath except in a few municipalities where the religious parties were not strongly represented. The Orthodox Rabbinate had and still has total control over births (circumcisions of males), marriage (no provisions for mixed marriages) and deaths (all burials are performed in the Jewish Orthodox mold). Jewish religious bodies such as the Conservative and Reform movements were not and still are not recognized.

Periodically during the existence of the Jewish State, government crises were brought about by the religious parties in the wake of challenges to them regarding the special concessions they had been granted by the government. These included the exemption from military service of women and male *Yeshiva* (religious seminary) students, and the provision of scholarships to these students.

Since no single party in the Israeli political system has been able to mount a majority in the *Knesset* (parliament), coalition government has been the rule. More often than not, one or more of the religious parties were called upon to join the government in order to attain the necessary numerical majority. That fact put them in a situation where their demands carried considerable leverage.

The disproportionate influence of a minority segment in the Israel parliament struck me as an unfortunate situation given the fact that the more fundamentalist parties among them rejected the idea of a secular democratic state—and still do. When I expressed the fear to an Israeli acquaintance that the society was moving in the direction of a theocracy he was most unsympathetic to the notion of "running away from the problem," as he put it. As a resident of the Jewish state, he pointed out, it would be my responsibility, like that of all like-minded, to fight for change.

Immediately upon settling in our first, unfortunate Jerusalem housing, we put finding jobs high on the agenda of activities. Our monetary reserves were limited and had to pay for housing, however modest, and food for two, and later, for the three of us. Shirley's job qualification included secretarial skills and experience and an Associate of Arts (two-year) degree from the Univerity of Minnesota. I had a Master's degree in sociology and psychology, also from Minnesota.

The state of Israel was barely two years old and in the process of filling government positions with a newly instituted Office of Civil Service. It was headed by an official who had run the civil service under British Mandatory auspices and an American professor, Sidney Mailick, who specialized in the study of civil service in the United States. The goal of this office was building an Israeli civil service based on a western model of hiring and promotion, resting on the merit system. How well did the system work during the early years of its existence? Our experience in the search for employment can give a few clues regarding the problems encountered when introducing new bureaucratic techniques into a society that has not embraced them in the past.

Shirley was a candidate for English secretary in the Ministry of the Treasury. I sought employment as a researcher in the Ministry of Welfare. For the former the applicant had to pass a test demonstrating knowledge of English, the ability to type and take shorthand. For the research position the requirement was proper credentials and an oral examination by a committee composed of academic social scientists. It is self-evident that the decision of the latter is more easily subject to interpretation and challenge than performance scores in typing and shorthand. Beyond that, the appointment of a professional who functions at a level of some independence poses more fundamental questions of suitability for a given work environment than does a typist, secretary or clerk.

Unlike Shirley who was offered the secretarial job for which she had applied and accepted, the Ministry of Social Welfare rejected my candidacy even though the civil service committee recommended me as the most qualified applicant. This rejection notwithstanding, I was allowed to fill the position temporarily without being given a hint regarding my future chances for long-term employment.

Several months later the research position in the Ministry was advertised once more. Again I presented myself as a candidate with the same results as before. Several weeks after this go-around the Director General of the ministry, Mr. Bar-Sela, called me to his office for an interview related to the still-vacant position. What followed gave me some understanding of what stood in the way of merit-based civil service testing.

The interview began with questions about my hometown, the birthplace of my parents, their later whereabouts, their ways of making a living, etc. The subsequent questions had to do with the issue of religiosity. (The ministry in which I worked was headed by Rabbi Yitzhak Meir Levine, the leader of one of the most rigorously Orthodox parties.) Mr. Bar-Sela wanted to know whether I was religious. The answer was negative. Is my wife religious? Again a negative response. I began to wonder what all these questions and answers had to do with my ability to carry out social research, but I held my tongue for fear of total rejection of my candidacy. What about my wife's parents? He spared my own family, being aware of the fact that my own parents were feared to have perished in Auschwitz (that was not confirmed till several years later). What about my wife's parents? Not really religious but traditional in observing holidays. What about their own parents? I finally hit pay dirt. The good man was clearly trying to help me. Shirley's grandfather was a *Chazan* (cantor) of an orthodox congregation in Minnesota, a highly religious man who studied Talmud on Saturday afternoons. The Director General made a note on his writing pad.

The conversation now shifted to Mannheim, the city in which I was born and raised. Did I know that Mannheim was the home of a famous rabbi named Unna? I did and quoted some of the works he had published. Was I aware that his son was a member of the Knesset (the Israeli parliament)? I was and cited his full name. Mr. Bar-Sela made a note of my last comment and ended the interview. Several weeks later, I was informed that the Ministry of Social Welfare had changed my temporary appointment to a permanent one.

In turning over in my mind this whole process, two thoughts occurred to me. First, a government service like the Ministry of Social Welfare that had come into being only two years earlier was likely to be suspicious of outsiders whose backgrounds existing members found hard to evaluate. A natural tendency is to appoint persons who are part of a familiar and political set. Secondly, in Israel's system of government—and for that matter, in that of the Jewish community operating under the auspices of the British Mandate—representing a nation in the process of becoming, ideological orientation assumes special importance as a key to power.

Mr. Bar-Sela directed his inquiry toward ascertaining that in social background and education I was not unlike the staff working under him. Such likeness included, of course, religious belief and in that respect I obviously fell short, but that shortcoming may have been overshadowed by the fact that during the time I had already worked at the ministry I had developed a positive track record.

The requirement of suitability, ideological, social and political, was not confined to the Ministry of Social Welfare or other ministries under religious auspices. When a research position was advertised in the Ministry of Labor, I applied and received top recommendations from the civil service office but was never considered for the position. I was unable to obtain information on the process or the outcome. Rumors had it that it was filled by an insider.

During the few months between our arrival in Jerusalem and my being hired by the Ministry of Social Welfare, I found employment as a Coordinator of Youth Services, a program operated by the Jerusalem Municipality. The youngsters were, with few exceptions, born in the Old City of Jerusalem and had to flee with their families when the Jordanian Arab Legion conquered that part of Jerusalem at the end of Israel's War of Independence. The boys and girls were referred to as abandoned youths, a term reflecting their status—considered socially deprived, tending toward delinquent behavior, and in a few instances mentally disturbed. A number of their families had been broken as a consequence of the war. Almost all of them were of Sephardic (Oriental Jewry) descent, generally considered of lower status than Ashkenazis (Western or Middle-European Jewry). They were faced with a new environment, very different from the Arab-like alleyways of the Old City, and with adjustment to a society unlike that from which they had come.

There were four group leaders who sought to involve their charges in sports, recreation, holiday celebrations, movies and cultural events. One of the favorite activities of the boys was watching war movies. The films reminded them of their roles in the War of Independence where they performed auxiliary functions supporting Israeli troops. One got the impression that participation in the war gave these young people a sense of importance that had been missing from their lives. Their parents, displaced from their homes, often unemployed, unaccustomed to the westernized society they were encountering, could not offer models for their children to follow. Our friend Nissan Hadas, one of the group leaders at the center, had a chance to stay in touch with several of the boys as they entered military service. He observed that they made a good transition into military life.

Work and study constituted an important part of our lives in Israel. As educated Americans we had hoped to make a positive contribution to the two-year-old Jewish state. Continuing my post-graduate work in sociology would hopefully add to my effectiveness as a researcher in the newly created society.

Shirley worked as an English secretary for the Secretary General at the Ministry of the Treasury until the birth of our first child, Layah, and then took two years off as a full-time housewife and baby-tender. She returned to work at a part-time position when we were able to place Layah during work hours with a neighbor who had a child the same age. The half-time position was secretary to the Israel representative of the International Labor Organization. My first full-time job was in the Department of Research and Planning of the Ministry of Social Welfare, first as researcher, later as Coordinator of Research.

The director of the department was a woman of German-Jewish origin, H. Gellner, who had held high-level administrative positions in the welfare system of the Jewish community in Palestine during the time of the British Mandate. Her guidelines for my assignments were vague, centering around the need to accumulate a library of relevant materials for future tasks which she did not define. As it turned out a major assignment came our way for writing a monograph on community organization and development in Israel. This work was part of a series of reports sponsored by the Social Commission of the United Nations.

The Department of Research and Planning had engaged another sociologist to collaborate on the project, Dr. Morton Rubin who had a Ph.D. from the University of North Carolina. We found the assignment very enjoyable. The country's wide experience with non-traditional forms of settlement and community organization made it a subject well worth reporting in an international forum. Mort Rubin and I utilized existing published materials and supplemented them with interviews of members of various forms of settlement. We submitted a draft of the study to Ms. Gellner, whose approval was needed before sending it on to the United Nations.

Although the deadline for submission was drawing near, we left ourselves enough time for revisions which would, of course, take into account the comments of our Department's head. However, nothing was forthcoming from her except a remark to the effect that we have to address the matter soon. By the time the day of the deadline arrived, Ms. Gellner had gone on a vacation to England without taking any action.

A telegram from Zena Harman, a member of Israel's delegation to the United Nations, addressed to the Director General of Israel's Ministry of Social Welfare, urged immediate action on our report. The hunt began for a copy of the document, and it ended quickly at the desk of Ms. Gellner where it had been locked in a drawer. I don't recall whether the drawer was broken open and the Gellner copy forwarded or whether Morton and I short circuited the process and sent our own copy to Ms. Harman directly. The fact remains that the Ministry did not turn the mismanaged situation into a cause celebre but urged our U.N. delegate to finalize the document. Needless to say Morton Rubin and I, who had closely followed Zena Harman's distinguished career, had full confidence in her ability to resolve the problem.

To the best of our knowledge the powers-that-be in the Ministry of Social Welfare had found no fault with Ms. Gellner's way of running her department. That was in contrast to her staff of researchers and secretaries who found her ways aloof, lacking respect for those working for her, and devoid of leadership (defined as identifying goals and jointly devising means to achieve them). She was particularly sensitive on the subject of her status and importance as a department head in a government ministry relative to other heads of organizations in the public arena. At one point during her directorship I invited Ms. Gellner to join me at a meeting regarding a research project at the office of a professor at the Hebrew University. She retorted sharply with the words, "I should go to the office of Professor so and so?" Obviously the professor did not, in her estimation, occupy a similarly exalted status; going to a venue below her own was not to be tolerated. She never asked about the substance of the meeting.

Several months after the predicament with the U.N. report a government crisis (I don't recall the precise issues) led to the resignation of the Minister of Social Welfare from his cabinet post. As is routine in situations of this kind the Prime Minister (at that time Ben Gurion) appointed himself as the acting head of the Ministry pending a resolution of the crisis. Other interim appointments included those of Director General and other top officials.

The staff of the department, reviewing the changes that were suddenly confronting us, reached the conclusion that the time was ripe to press for changes in the directorship. I volunteered to be part of a small delegation that would seek an appointment with the acting Director General. This was scheduled on short notice. The person, a woman whose name escapes me, listened to our complaint sympathetically and told us that she was fully aware of the problems we had cited. However, due to the fact that Ms. Gellner had been a pioneer in the field of Jewish welfare, going back to the days of the British Mandate, there was no way in which the government of Israel could in good conscience terminate her services. Thanking the Director General for her courtesy in receiving us, we saw the meeting as the end, however unsuccessful, of our mission.

Imagine our surprise when we learned that Ms. Gellner had been informed by an undisclosed person about our audience and, without a moment's delay, wrote a letter of resignation. This, it appears, was followed by an equally expeditious "acceptance with regret" on behalf of the Government of Israel. Within hours there was a public announcement making the resignation official. We can only speculate about the dynamic underlying these developments, because nobody revealed the actual facts to us.

Ms. Gellner, a stickler for formality, must never have thought of herself as being vulnerable. It was inconceivable to her that her underlings would openly revolt against her administrative conduct and go over her head to negotiate with her superiors. Or more outrageously, that the acting heads of the Ministry would give serious consideration to the claims of a rebel group. Above all, she must have been convinced that her past achievements and present status guaranteed her immunity from attack by elements that failed to measure up to her level of importance. Clearly, Ms. Gellner acted impulsively being fully convinced that no high ranking official in his or her right mind would approve of an egregious violation of the bureaucratic process such as the one in which we had engaged. If this argument guided her thinking it was proceeding close to the truth. Unfortunately for her she really believed that in her position as Director of Research and Planning she was irreplaceable. On that score—which led her to hand in her resignation—she was out of touch with reality.

H. Gellner's replacement was Dr. Efrat, former director of Meir *Shefayah*, a well-known Center for Youth *Aliyah* (a program to settle and train Jewish youth in Palestine and Israel) composed of young people who had arrived from countries of the Diaspora often without their parents or close relatives. This appointment represented a significant change for the better for members of the department and ultimately for the work we were hired to do. Dr. Efrat had no formal training as a social researcher. However, he had a keen grasp of the issues we were struggling with whether in the form of social surveys or reporting on some aspects of social institutions and community development in the framework of international data collection. He was always accessible to staff and had an open, confidence-inspiring way of evaluating performance and results. He always made sure that all contributors to studies and reports were given credit for their work, a principle too often disregarded by bureaucratic systems. Speaking for myself, work took on a new meaning and added satisfaction under the directorship of Dr. Efrat.

One aspect of our life in Israel was problem-ridden from the start as reported above. It continued to pose difficulties for the first two and a half years of our stay in the country. We found it impossible to continue renting a room with the baker and his wife who could not tolerate a colicky baby nor the constant washing and bottle-making that necessitated considerable sharing of the kitchen. We began an urgent search for better quarters. The shortage of housing in the country made it necessary to pay a hefty sum in key money (compensation under the table) in addition to the rental fee. Sale of our used car gave us only a little leeway for upgrading our housing conditions. (By the way, the key money arrangement was widespread in Western society during and following World War II, when it was not considered legal but generally tolerated. That was the case in Israel as well.)

The property we rented, or more precisely purchased with key money, comprised two rooms in a building that sat astride of the Old City wall. Until the withdrawal of the British from Palestine this edifice was known as the Hotel Fast or *Malon Fast* in Hebrew. It was a billet for members of the British armed forces and also a center for recreation. The building was badly damaged during the War of Independence, which left the Jordanian Army, known as the Arab Legion, in possession of the Old City while Israel held on to the New City and the surrounding suburbs. The legal owner of Malon Fast was the Russian Orthodox Church whose headquarters were in the so-called Russian compound located in the New City.

The agent who arranged the sale fed us some misinformation regarding the toilet facilities that went with the apartment. Although located across the hall from the flat they were supposed to be private, i.e., reserved exclusively for our use. What we found was an Arab squat toilet, one of three off a dark corridor, and we quickly converted it into a European type with a tank suspended above the commode. Israelis refer to this type as a *niagarah*, a bastardization of Niagara, the world's ultimate flush. To secure the privacy of the privy, we attached a padlock to the door.

Imagine our surprise when an attempted use of the facilities revealed another padlock which did not yield to our key. A short investigation with informed neighbors revealed that our toilet was being used by customers and the owners of a kiosk serving fast food and drinks, located in another section of the Malon. Israeli law requires that customers of food establishments must have access to toilet facilities. Fair enough especially when you remember that in the United States the physical needs of customers are often neglected in fast food places, filling stations, and even small bus and train depots. This observation, however, is small consolation in the face of the fact that we had rented and paid for an apartment with private toilet facilities.

There was nothing in writing legalizing the agreement between the landlord and the owner of the kiosk or the occupier of the apartment as to sharing toilet facilities. Given the situation we decided to pursue our interests by means of direct action. Stage one: Cut the padlock installed by the kiosk with a metal saw and replace it with our own. Results: Successive destruction and removal of the other party's padlock served no one but the manufacturers of padlocks. Stage two: Report the conflict to the local police. They responded by arranging a meeting between the contending sides in the course of which a pep talk by a police sergeant was followed by his advice to shake hands and forget about the whole problem. Results: Both parties rejected the advice and walked away in opposite directions. Stage three: A trip to the offices of the Russian Orthodox Church, Malon Fast's landlord. Results: A sympathetic hearing given by an official of the church who ended the meeting by saying, "Get a good lawyer to handle the case."

In retrospect, our not winning the case of the private privy probably worked to our advantage. It strengthened our case when applying for government-subsidized housing as will be explained later. In the meantime, we struggled with the ongoing problem of living in unhygienic conditions which were of special concern because of Layah, still an infant but soon to be a toddler.

There were inherent problems with Malon Fast. The building was damaged and possibly structurally unsound as a result of having been a defensive outpost for the Israeli Army during the recent war. The people now occupying the building were immigrants from underdeveloped countries in the Middle East and eastern Europe. They lived under crowded conditions, sometimes eight, ten or more in a single room. Clogged flush toilets were a constant problem in the building because of improper use as well as poor plumbing. (When I became aware of the trouble, I appointed myself "community developer" going from room to room and explaining the correct use of the toilets and collecting money for paying the plumber.)

Our own sanitary facilities were most unsatisfactory. Although we had installed a *niagarah*, it was reached after walking down a dark hallway across from our doorway, past three cells each containing an open-pit Arab toilet. There was no electricity to light the way. And the main hallway (which must have been the hotel lobby in better days) which led down a small passageway to our rooms was often used by the little Iraqi children from other first-floor rooms to defecate when they were too busy playing to return to their own rooms.

Aside from the above, our two rooms at the hotel were a step above the norm in the building. Once you crossed the outer lobby and maneuvered down the dim hallway you entered a small kitchen with a sink (which we had installed) and behind glass doors could find a bathtub on a raised platform. The living room to the right was sparsely furnished with a couch, a crib, a table, chairs and a cabinet. Our flat had obviously served some other purpose when the British army held sway and the bathtub may have been the only one in the place. Friends of Mollie and Henry Weiller who had played surrogate parents to me when I first arrived in Saint Paul, sounded the alarm about our style of living. Mollie wrote to us that there would be some money waiting for us any time we are ready to accept their gift. However, Shirley and I thought we were staying afloat for the present, but that in due time we would welcome better accommodations.

Historically, the area around our residence, located at the Old City wall, was close to landmarks held sacred by three religions. What stared us in the face, however, were the consequences of the recent war for the Kingdom of Jordan blocked Jewish access to any of the religious or archeologically interesting sites. From a more prosaic vantage point, even hanging laundry on the flat roof of the Malon posed a risk because the Arab Legionnaires patrolled the top of the wall, a stone's throw away, and one could never be sure how a guard would react to the enemy across the way. Shirley reported at least one occasion when a guard whistled at her, but there were many more reported instances of shooting than friendly or sexually appreciative gestures. Many were the times when the street between the Malon and the Wall had to be abandoned because Legionnaires were firing at pedestrians.

The first-floor neighbors with whom we shared the Malon were recent immigrants from the Middle East. Upstairs were also recent immigrants, but these were from regions of Central Europe, probably uprooted refugees from WW II, many of whom were Orthodox. There was almost no contact between the two groups and very little sympathy for each other. All of the families had spent some time in a Maabarah after coming to Israel—that is, an immigrant transit camp made up of corrugated iron-roofed huts—and found the more protected, urban quarters near Jerusalem's center a decided improvement. Our communication with them was limited because few of them spoke a language we could handle, neither Hebrew, English, German nor a bit of French. One contact, however, stands out because language was not needed and the message was clear. Shortly after moving in, Shirley had gone to the roof to hang laundry, leaving the baby alone in the rooms. She returned to find a Kurdish woman in the apartment, cradling and rocking Layah, who had been crying. The woman had heard the baby cry and, as luck would have it, found the door open. Her message was clear: Shirley had done the unforgivable, namely, letting the baby cry. She demonstrated excitedly what needed to be done to pacify the infant. Shirley thanked her profusely with gestures, realizing that she had done the unforgivable by Kurdish or Iraqi child-rearing rules. As we thought about the impromptu lesson, we came to the conclusion that we seldom heard babies crying in the Malon even though there were many scattered throughout the first floor. We later observed that Middle Eastern women took their infants with them wherever they went and sometimes employed hammocks as a means of rocking small children to sleep. Although the women kept to their work, the infants were always nearby and soothed.

Our stay at Malon Fast exceeded a year until we were close to the time when Layah would begin to walk. We felt some urgency about moving to a home that provided a cleaner environment and some outdoor space where she could play. The problem centered around our ability to finance such a move. A single idea occurred to me which I thought worth pursuing although it might not constitute a convincing argument—requesting help from the government. Mindful of Prime Minister Ben Gurion's appeal for immigrants from Western societies, I decided to send him a letter describing our motivation of making *Aliyah* (come to the Jewish homeland) and our housing predicament. I posted the letter without asking for prior advice from anyone, but shared my deed with Shirley after the fact. Her response was brief and to the point: "It was a crackpot thing to do." I didn't actually expect a reply, anticipating that the matter would be handled at the lowest bureaucratic echelon if at all. Imagine my surprise when I received a letter within a week from the Office of the Prime Minister asking me to meet with his representative. I was even more astounded when it turned out that the representative was Ehud Avriel, the Director General (and the number two man) in the Prime Minister's Office and a leading figure in the history of the Jewish State. It was Ehud Avriel who was a key person in organizing illegal Jewish immigration before statehood and in arming Israel in the face of the invasion of Arab states after the declaration of the State of Israel.

Mr. Avriel told me that the Prime Minister regretted

not being present and acknowledged the concerns expressed in my letter. He asked me to keep in mind that when he himself came to Palestine his mode of housing had been a chicken coop. I said that was *then*, and things had changed quite a bit in the meantime. He asked me about the work I was doing at the Ministry of Social Welfare and made several critical remarks about it, the details of which I do not remember. I pointed out that I had been hired to do research, not to make policy. The interview ended by Mr. Avriel saying he would see what he could do for me. Not many days later Mr. Noy, the Secretary General of the Ministry of Social Welfare, called me with the thrilling information that we had been placed on a waiting list for government housing and that we could probably count on resettling in the near future. There was no doubt that the Welfare Ministry had given strong support to our quest for improved housing. To make the situation even better, an opportunity arose for us to temporarily rent the apartment of a rabbi returning to the U.S., Rabbi Walter Plaut, who was the former director of Herzl Camp in Wisconsin where both Shirley and I had worked as counselors. Needless to say, we jumped at the opportunity without delay. And so we moved into a two-bedroom apartment replete with electricity, a refrigerator, a natural gas stove and an in-house toilet, boasting furniture, a balcony and a garden where Layah could learn to walk without concern regarding hygiene or safety.

Living in Israel as a permanent resident in the years following the birth of the state posed problems which could be termed status ambiguities, problems to a large extent the result of low tolerance in the U.S. for multiple citizenship. The legal aspects of this problem were complicated and have undergone changes over time. I shall deal with the subject mainly in terms of our own experience. The problems did not arise from my status as a naturalized American since legislation following World War II conferred citizenship on veterans like myself as a result of army service, and extended to us the same rights possessed by native-born Americans.

The Israeli Law of Return bestowed automatic citizenship on any Jewish person, coming from abroad with the desire of settling in Israel. That carried with it the obligation to serve in the armed forces. In keeping with this law I signed up for reserve duty that included military activity one day a month at a nearby army installation and a month of full-time duty, generally away from home. Within about a year of my joining the Israeli Army, the government of the United States informed its citizens living in Israel that the service we were rendering was in violation of our status as American citizens. The implication was clearly that continued service for Israel could lead to loss of United States citizenship.

The government of Israel, being obviously aware that requiring the military service of Americans could lead to their exodus, gave them the option of being released from service. I selected that option for myself. (Later in time I volunteered to give a week's service near the Gaza strip which was then held by Egypt. The assignment was under civilian not military auspices.) The legal basis for the American edict was anything but clear. Citizens of this country have rendered military service to a friendly nation such as England and Canada prior to our entry into World War II. Again, the Israeli War of Independence attracted American volunteers who included Colonel David "Mickey" Marcus, a U.S. army officer and West

Point graduate. I am not aware that he or any other American volunteers were ever threatened with a loss of citizenship.

We as a family now numbering three had our own problems with the American Consular Service in Israel. The official in charge at the Jerusalem office was a woman by the name of Sara McDonald. She registered the birth of our first child, Layah, for citizenship without any problem. But weeks later when I came to extend our passports whose expiration dates were just a few days away, she asked all kinds of intrusive questions such as did I have any jobs in addition to being a Ph.D. student (I worked then part-time for the Jerusalem municipality as an Activities Coordinator), the nature of our housing and how long did we plan to stay in the country. I resisted by saying that her questions were not relevant to our request for passport extension. She countered that she was not ready to extend our passports at this time. When she refused to give any reason, I said I would contact our U.S. Senator in Minnesota and complain about her inaction. Her reaction was immediate and physical. She pushed me out of the door.

An American acquaintance of ours who about that time came to register her child Sarah reported the following comments a propos that name: "In the south where I come from, Sarah is a nice upstanding name. But in New York, they give the name Sarah only to Jews."

On two future occasions when we required passport extensions we employed two alternatives to avoid future harassment. We went to the American consulate in Tel Aviv and also used the Jerusalem office when Sara McDonald was on vacation. In the wake of the expulsion scene witnessed by another consulate worker, I got all the cooperation I needed when hostile Sara was safely out of the way.

Other than housing and the strained relationship with the Consulate, life in Jerusalem moved in its normal channels. Under the leadership of Dr. Efrat my assignments in the Department of Research and Planning comprised writing reports for the United Nations and affiliated bodies on aspects of social and economic developments in Israel. The U.N. endeavors were part of a larger international effort to provide and exchange information for the benefit of member nations. Another aspect of my work required the collection of information for visiting dignitaries known as experts commissioned to critique aspects of Israeli institutions and services. Finally, Dr. Efrat reviewed my Ph.D. program and concluded that certain aspects were relevant to the work of the department and could be pursued during my work hours.

My Ph.D. work in sociology at the Hebrew University took on a central role in our life in Jerusalem. Our plan to live in Israel was contingent on attaining an advanced degree and, hopefully, employment in academia. My Ph.D. committee was chaired by Professor S.N. Eisenstadt, head of the Department of Sociology, and Professors Yisrael Halperin and Jacob Katz of the Departments of History, giving consideration to the fact that the thesis had basic historical dimensions.

The study was designed to examine the influence of immigrants' ideology on their adjustment to life in Israel. The distinction was drawn between newcomers who left their countries of origin voluntarily and free from external pressures and those who were forced to leave because of anti-Semitism or repressive social and political conditions. The study was confined to educated immigrants working for the government, studying at the university or living in a Kibbutz (collective settlement). Data collection required interviews with subjects in different parts of the country. A research grant from Professor Eisenstadt enabled me to train interviewers as well as carry out a content analysis of the Zionist organs in the countries of origin regarding the nature of motivational influences leading to a migration to Israel.

At one point in my work on the dissertation, a positive event interfered with my efforts to hurry it along. The reader will remember that the government had added our names to a list for newly constructed housing. Now, the apartment was at last available. As we got ready to move we learned that the apartment in suburban Katamon (a Jerusalem suburb) would not be connected to the electric network for some weeks. In point of fact, it actually took some thirty weeks. We welcomed, of course, the better environment, a second floor apartment of our own on the edge of a field studded with wild flowers and a low, subsidized rent to boot. But reading, executing statistical calculations and writing under the light of a kerosene lamp were not exactly conducive to scholarly productivity. Still and all, the absence of externally imposed deadlines made the conditions bearable, and we both agreed that our standard of living had been appreciably raised.

As time went on, assignments in the Department of Research and Planning under the direction of Dr. Efrat took on deeper meaning for they were carried out in an atmosphere of freedom of inquiry. He encouraged us to enlarge our sources of information and to cross political boundaries, if necessary, to get at pertinent facts.

One of the more intriguing assignments involved my participation in a United Nations Study Tour of Community Organizations in selected member nations. This endeavor built on a resolution of the U.N. Social and Economic Council to compile information on community organization and development. Underlying this program was the belief that community organization is an important concept in social and economic development of human societies.

The particular study tour in which I was privileged to participate as an Israeli representative (more specifically, of the Ministry of Social Welfare) was composed of five countries, namely, Greece, Iran, Israel, Turkey and Yugoslavia. The aggregation of these five requires some explanation. It represented a compromise of the approach favored by the Social and Economic Council of the U.N., that of selecting study countries that were located in a specific geographic area. Such an approach can be justified by the fact that adjacent countries tend to be similar in social and economic development and the propinquity could encourage the instituting of programs on an area-wide basis. But for obvious political reasons, the idea of an area-wide program was totally unacceptable to Israel's Arab neighbors. The borders of Israel were protected at best by armistice agreements, and one neighbor, Iraq, which had completely refused to sign an agreement, was still officially at war with the Jewish State. In order for Israel to be a participant in a multi-nation project, the U.N. created a study group composed of the five nations listed above, disregarding the lack of a shared geography. Two of the five countries, Iran and Turkey, were predominantly Muslim in religious orientation, and that fact forced certain limitations on participation and on their representatives' conduct vis-a-vis Israel. Thus, the countries would not agree to serve as study sites that could be visited by tour members and their representatives were not allowed to visit Israel. Although the Iranian and Turkish delegations requested of their governments to permit Israeli visits—the Israeli government was willing to forgo the stamping of passports—the requests were denied.

The director of the tour was Charles Alspach, Director of the U.N. Division of Community Organization. He was an American with a social work background, an outgoing personality, and very much at ease in his leadership role. The participating countries were asked to send four-member delegations representing the areas of education, health, social welfare and agriculture or rural development. The head of the Israeli delegation was Dr. J. Yaphe, a physician and Deputy Director General of Israel's Ministry of Health. There was an expectation that delegates were involved in policy development and execution in their respective countries. For purposes of the study tour they were expected to be fluent in either English or French, the languages used by the interpreters who translated information from the native tongues of the countries visited. There was but one woman among the delegates, Mrs. O. Vrabic, a member of the Yugoslavian Federal People's Assembly (national parliament) and also of the Executive Council of Slovenia.

The study tour, which lasted nearly a month, was an unusual and interesting experience for me. I can summarize but a few memories as best. The host nations, Yugoslavia, Greece and Israel, made every effort to roll out the red carpet, with each country attempting to trump the preceding one that was visited in hospitality and generosity.

Initial formality in relations among the delegations

gave rise to a more relaxed stance during the trip, particularly on the long bus trips through the Yugoslavian countryside. Nothing lightened the atmosphere as much as bathroom stops where there were no bathrooms (but a routine of hiding behind bushes) and the mutual aid practiced when a new bus began leaking in several places during a rainstorm. In the respective countries visited, receptions were held by leading personalities and government officials. In Israel, Prime Minister Moshe Sharet personally received the delegates. Relations among the various members were informal even in situations in which the respective governments had set limitations. In briefings in Israel prior to the tour, we had been cautioned to be circumspect since listening devices were often planted in hotel rooms. We found no evidence of their use. We were surprised, however, by the fact that on several occasions during the Yugoslavian tour, civilians would speak to us quite openly about perceived problems in their country without seeming fear of retribution. In Greece, by contrast, delegates of the study tour would seldom find themselves going anywhere without being accompanied by the local senior politician, police representative and clergyman. This all happened during the period that is known as the "era of the colonels."

The study tour was a trove of experiences that provided delegates with glimpses of life in geographically and ethnically diverse settings. It highlighted institutions and programs that could be utilized to further community development (Yugoslavia and Israel put special emphasis on collective modes of living). Delegates of the countries we could not visit, Iran and Turkey, sought to convey to us pictures of societies that were change-oriented and open to ideas of reform. This was particularly pronounced in the accounts of the Iranians who depicted Shah Palevi as pushing programs for modernization to improve social and economic conditions. This trend, if it were indeed genuine, was brought to a halt by the bloody revolution of the mullahs under the leadership of Ayatolla Khomeini.

The general ambiance among the delegations was cordial, and the cool attitude of the Turkish and Iranian regimes toward Israel did not express itself in interpersonal relationships. Differences, if any, had more to do with definitions of concepts. When the Yugoslavs used the term social, it invariably comprised the economic dimension in keeping with Marxian usage which ascribes economic motives and goals to all social behavior. Adequate knowledge of a common second language could be a barrier to communication. Mrs. Vrabic of the Yugoslavian delegation, a former partisan fighter in WW II, sought to compare our experiences under the Nazi regime but for similar emotional reasons resisted speaking German. Our knowledge of French was too limited for free-flowing conversation. It was not until the Yugoslav's departure from Israel that we both broke down and conversed in German for a mutual understanding of our respective experiences in a world that had come apart.

The study tour for me was a unique experience that fell into my lap, so to speak, because the Israeli official who headed the Department of Community Organization was thought to be too "controversial." By the same token, the tour—however interesting—made me realize that my future was not in diplomacy. My experience of the past years, both in the United States and Israel, was anchored in efforts aimed at knowledge building that relied on the use of social science research techniques. I derived greater satisfaction from the quest after truth and sharing it with others than from the more glittering activity and lifestyle of diplomacy.

In the fall of 1956, Professor Eisenstadt arranged for me to teach a course in Introductory Sociology and Anthropology at Tel Aviv University. The classes were held at night in temporary quarters, since the university was still engaged in building its own campus. The ride back to Jerusalem at night on an inter-city bus was less relaxing than it might have been because of the periodic attacks by Arab marauders on routes running through unsettled areas or close to the border. Terrorism targeting Jewish life and property had been part of life in Palestine and Israel since the start of Jewish settlement more than a century before, but in the autumn of '56 it seemed to have accelerated.

Much of the preceding fall and the early spring of 1956 was devoted to making the final corrections on my Ph.D. dissertation and waiting for the doctoral committee's review as well as the University Senate's approval of the work. The title was Zionist Ideology Among Young Immigrants to Israel. Defense of the dissertation, which went smoothly, was accompanied by a bit of clever graffiti scratched on the program posted for announcement purposes in the lobby of Terra Santa (the building that was rented from the Vatican where the defense took place). It slyly said: "Long live the Doctor of Zionism." This witticism must be understood against the background of cynicism that had developed among the younger generation of native-born Israelis in the fifties who were future-oriented and contemptuous of the past, including the Diaspora and the Zionism it generated. A common expression of this period was "Don't stuff my brain with Zionism."

The author of the graffiti was obviously poking at someone—me—aspiring to be the doctor of Zionism.

In December of 1955 our second daughter, Deborah, was born. By that time Layah was four years old and attending pre-kindergarten. At Passovertime Shirley and our two children flew to the United States to attend the wedding of her younger sister Rochelle. I stayed behind until May in order to complete teaching my course in Tel Aviv.

At the time of our departure no final decision had been made whether to return to Israel or resettle in the United States. Shirley favored the former, influenced by the close bonds we had formed in Israel and a feeling of obligation to help in the task of rebuilding the Jewish homeland. As it turned out, an appointment as Research Director of the St. Paul Family Centered Project, a nationally known social welfare research-action endeavor, followed three years later by a tenure position at Rutgers University in New Jersey, paved the way for relocating, making our permanent home once more in the United States.

Afterword

The most significant event during the second half of the twentieth century was the breakup of the Soviet Union, leaving the United States as the sole superpower on the face of the earth. The collapse of the so-called communist society was read in the West, but particularly the United States, as the ultimate evidence of the bankruptcy of all the isms of the left, which in American political language frequently includes liberalism.

The absence of a deliberate ideology in the American political landscape, referred to in the Preface, is best illustrated in the campaign strategy of President George W. Bush which calls for winning reelection at all cost but omits or downplays specific goals for the nation. To the extent that goals are mentioned, they are derived from a close reading of the latest public opinion polls.

In the Bush case, this goal flexibility is, nevertheless, matched by a firm belief in Christian fundamentalism. In fairness to him, it should be pointed out that American electioneering as a whole plays down adherence to ideology in favor of personality and general appearance in the media. This is aided by the fact that the American voter tends to support middle of the roaders who avoid unknown ideological territory.

One of the major realignments after the demise of the Soviet Union was the thrust toward extreme nationalism both secular and mixed with religion or quasi-Marxism. Northern Ireland, India-Pakistan, Vietnam, Palestine,

Sri Lanka, Iran, Iraq, African regions, and Afghanistan are some of the best-known sites of conflict during the last half century. When the two superpowers, the United States and the Soviet Union, confronted each other they operated under a general agreement, backed by treaties, to reduce nuclear stockpiles and take other measures to avoid a catastrophic confrontation. The need for such measures had become particularly acute in the wake of the nuclear missile crisis in 1962.

Ideally the new age of detente among the world's leading powers should have led to an era of peace and security. Instead, the world has been plagued by regional wars resulting in the loss of countless lives and destruction of properties on a global scale. The modes of conflict utilize mass terror that knows no borders and resorts to suicidal attacks such as the bombing of the World Trade Towers on September 11, 2001 and the Intifata in Palestine/Israel. The common denominator of these struggles is a firm conviction on the part of the contenders that their values, beliefs, and way of life are the only valid ones and can be attained solely by the use of violence. Such claims are, of course, not a product of the twentieth or twenty-first centuries thinking but have underlain most wars and conflicts in human history. What is new, however, is the self-sacrificing modes of attack, which disregard the lives of friend and foe alike.

One would have thought that the wide prevalence of ultra-nationalistic and religious struggles would have given rise to universal condemnation, as a principle of world culture and civilized behavior and as a field of political action on the part of the United Nations. Such has indeed not occurred. Instead, national religious extremism has served to divide the world along the lines of diverse political causes. Taking sides became mainly a matter of assuming a position which would best serve the interests of the parties that felt impelled to take a stand.

The positions being taken by the contending parties in a conflict are seldom a matter in which one side or the other has all the right on their side. The Israel-Palestine controversy with which I am most familiar may serve as a case in point. If one can agree to select as a starting point the United Nations action to resolve the problem with the expired British Mandate over Palestine, a number of events can be cited to gain a perspective on the issue. It is not helpful to start with narratives of the Bible or the Muslim conquests or the Crusades or the rule of the Ottoman and British empires to bolster the case. Nor is citing the Will of God an argument that will lead to a rational resolution.

In November 1947, the General Assembly of the United Nations, following action by the Security Council, voted for the partition of Palestine into Jewish and Arab states. On January 15, 1948, the Arab League announced that the armies of its eight members would occupy all of Palestine when the British withdraw in May 1948. Even prior to their complete evacuation, seven Arab armies started their invasion to make good on their January promise. The ensuing war, known in Israel as the War of Independence, and three further armed conflicts between the Arab states and Israel had as their Arab declared goal driving Israel into the sea. A fourth armed encounter was the Suez War in 1956 when Israel joined Britain and France in a battle to lift the Egyptian-imposed blockade of the Suez Canal.

Perhaps the greatest opportunity for peace since the U.N. partition of Palestine arose in the wake of the Oslo accords when U.S. President Bill Clinton hosted peace negotiations at Camp David. The meetings resulted in failure when far-reaching territorial concessions by Israel's Prime Minister Ehud Barak were rejected by the president of the Palestine Authority, Yasir Arafat. His answer was resumption of the Intifata with a new strategy—the use of suicide bombers against civilian targets.

It would be a mistake to describe the situation entirely in terms of Israel's good will and Arab rejectionism. The government of Prime Minister Sharon, presently in power, brings together segments of the Israeli populations whose beliefs leave no room for co-existence, religious diversity, separation of creed (church) and state, and other principles of democratic society. Collectively, they represent a minority of the populace, but in a political system composed of numerous parties none of which come close to having a numerical majority the influence of deviant minorities is substantial. Israel can hardly be proud of having one of its own citizens assassinate its popular Prime Minister Yitzhak Rabin or have one of the leaders of West Bank settlements, Dr. Baruch Goldstein, massacre Arabs at prayer. On the subject of settlements, Israel has been facing justified criticism for establishing new ones after agreements had been reached to halt such activities.

Still and all, the case for a Jewish state—beside a Palestinian state if so desired—is clear-cut. The United Nations supported the endeavor, and the need for a Jewish homeland was strongly underlined by the occurrence of the Holocaust and the existence of a vast number of displaced Jews.

Sixty-five years have passed since the murder of my brother in Dachau, and sixty years had elapsed since my parents were gassed to death in Auschwitz. My sister Hedy and I had lived with the uncertainty about their fate until Serge and Beate Klarsfeld (1983), well-known Nazi hunters, published a book on the deportations of Jews from France and West Germany. This volume contained the names and other identification of our parents and nine close relatives who had suffered the same fate. The disheartening distance of these events impeded efforts to remember and commemorate. That condition, as noted in the Preface, was suddenly altered in the summer of 2003 with an invitation from Dr. Walesch-Schneller of Breisach am Rhein, to join her group for a memorial assembly to commemorate the deportations of Jews including my parents on October 22, 1940. This group is known as the Association for the Restoration of Jewish Life which had in prior years rebuilt the Gemeindehaus or Jewish Center and cleaned and restored the Jewish cemetery. The Gemeindehaus served as a religious sanctuary after the Nazis torched the synagogue on *Kristallnacht*. Other efforts of the Association included promoting education, particularly among high school and college students, aimed at awareness of the Nazi past and perpetual efforts to prevent their reemergence.

In January 2004 Dr. Walesch-Schneller's work received twofold national recognition: She was given the Obermayer German Jewish History award for outstanding contributions to preserving and recording Jewish history, heritage, culture and/or remnants of local German communities. She was furthermore honored at a reception by the President of Germany Johannes Rau for distinguished services as a citizen.

During my stay in Germany, I had the opportunity to meet with students and adult groups in the Freiburg-

Breisach area. Most of them had volunteered time and resources for the Association. They were eager to hear from me as an eyewitness, and their questions revealed a sincere interest in the tragic events of the past. For me, the visit in the company of my wife Shirley and my brother-in-law, Melvin, husband of my late sister Hedy, opened a long-delayed chapter of connectedness in my life. It served as a bridge enabling me to span the dreadful void of the Holocaust and pay tribute to my loved ones.

Bibliography

Avineri, Shlomo (1981) *The Making of Modern Zionism*, London: Weidenfeld and Nicolson.
Axinn, June and Levin, Herman. (1975) *Social Welfare: A History of the American Response to Need*. New York: Dodd, Mead, and Company.
Bauer, Yehuda (1982) *A History of the Holocaust*. Danbury, CT: Franklin Watts.
Bell, Daniel (1962) *The End of Ideology*. New York: The Free Press.
Burg, David F. (1998) *Encyclopedia of Student and Youth Movements*. New York: Facts on File.
Clausen, John (1959) "The Sociology of Mental Illness," in Merton, Robert, Brown, Leonard, and Cottrell, Leonard S. Jr. *Sociology Today*. New York: Basic Books, Inc. pp.485–508.
Eisenstadt, S.N. (1971) *From Generation to Generation: Age Groups and Social Structure*. New York: The Free Press.
Encyclopaedia Britannica (1962) World War II Encyclopaedia vol. 23. pp. 790–793S.
Geismar, Ludwig L. (1954) "A Scale for the Measurement of Ethnic Identification." *Jewish Social Studies*, 16 pp.33–60.
Geismar, Ludwig L. (1959) "Ideology and the Adjustment

of Immigrants." *Jewish Social Studies*, 21 pp. 155–164.

Gribetz, Judah, with Greenstein, Edward L. and Stein, Regina S. (1994) *The Timetables of Jewish History*. New York: Touchstone Book, Simon and Schuster.

Kahane, Reuven (1997) *The Origins of Postmodern Youth. Informal Movements in a Comparative Perspective*. New York: Walter de Gruiter.

Klarsfeld, Serge (1983) *Memorial to the Jews Deported From France*. New York: Beate Klarsfeld Foundation.

Laqueur, Walter Z. (2001) *Generation Exodus: The Fate of Young Jewish Refugees from Nazi Germany*. Hanover, NH: University Press of New England.

Laqueur, Walter Z. (1962) *Young Germany: A History of the German Youth Movement*. New York: Basic Books Publishing Co. Inc.

Lewin, Kurt (1945) *Resolving Social Conflicts*. New York: Harper & Brothers.

Lewis, Sinclair (1935) *It Can't Happen Here*. New York: Collier & Son.

Oppenheimer, Franz (1926) *Der Staat* (The State-English Edition): New Brunswick, NJ: Transaction Books 1999.

Parsons, Talcott (1951) *The Social System*. New York: Glencoe.

Preil, Joseph J. (ed) (2001) *Holocaust Testimonies. European Survivors and American Liberators in New Jersey*. New Brunswick, NJ: Rutgers University Press.

Statchura, Peter D. (1981) *The German Youth Movement 1900–1945*. New York: St. Martin's Press.

Waxman, Chaim Isaac (ed) (1968) *The End of Ideology Debate*. New York: Funk and Wagnalls.

Willkie, Wendell L. (1943) *One World*. New York: Simon and Schuster.
Zucotti, Susan (1999) *The Holocaust, The French, and the Jews,* Lincoln: University of Nebraska Press.